No Sew Love

50 FUN PROJECTS TO MAKE WITHOUT A NEEDLE AND THREAD

ASHLEY JOHNSTON

CREATOR OF MAKEIT-LOVEIT.COM

RUNNING PRESS
PHILADELPHIA · LONDON

This book will always be dedicated to my sweet little ones Elliana, Connor, and Chloe, who inspire my creativity and shower their momma with love. And to my ever patient husband, Steve. I love you dearly.

Books published by Running Press are available at special discounts for bulk purchases in the United States by corporations, institutions, and other organizations. For more information, please contact the Special Markets Department at the Perseus Books Group, 2300 Chestnut Street, Suite 200, Philadelphia, PA 19103, or call (800) 810-4145, ext. 5000, or e-mail special.markets@perseusbooks.com.

ISBN 978-0-7624-5106-7
Library of Congress Control Number: 2013951592

E-book ISBN 978-0-7624-5532-4

9 8 7 6 5 4 3 2 1
Digit on the right indicates the number of this printing

Cover and interior design by Ashley Haag
Edited by Kristen Green Wiewora
Typography: Lobster Two, Benton Sans, and Avenir

Running Press Book Publishers
2300 Chestnut Street
Philadelphia, PA 19103-4371

Visit us on the web!
www.runningpress.com

ACKNOWLEDGMENTS

To the incredibly supportive and caring people who stop by and read my blog, Make It and Love It. From the very beginning, I have been astounded by the support, encouragement, and excitement provided by you dear friends. I can't even tell you how fulfilling you have made this strange little world we call "blogland" for me. I'm serious about the "all readers welcome" party that I want to throw one of these days!

To my family and friends who helped me pick between fabric "A" and "B," played "tea party" with my kids while I finished one last book edit, quickly smiled when I said we'd be having cereal for dinner . . . again, told me it was perfectly okay to let the laundry pile up, and buoyed me up when I needed you most. Thank you all.

To Katherine, who saw a vision for me, bigger than I could have imagined. And wow, how you've encouraged me!

To Kristen, who showed an abundant amount of patience for a momma with young children. Every new author needs an editor equally as loving!

To Elli, Connor, Chloe, Christine, Lauren, Emma, Jake, and Brielle for modeling your little hearts out for me. You are beautiful people, inside and out!

To the creators of those no-sew supplies out there for sale. It's shocking, but you really can do so much without a needle and thread!

And lastly, a huge thanks to my loving husband, Steve, for giving me wings to fly and telling me that my dreams are always worth it.

Contents

INTRODUCTION

A whole book packed with projects . . . and not a single one requires a sewing machine? *You got it!*

I know what you're thinking. You're probably wondering if I'm being sneaky and have hidden a few steps that "suggest" using a machine. Or maybe that several projects include at least a bit of hand sewing, with a needle and thread. Go ahead and leaf through the book, I'll wait for you . . . but you won't find a single thread sewn into any of these projects.

In fact, anyone can pick up this book and create the projects inside! And why would they? Because making things with your own two hands brings a great deal of satisfaction, eliciting that lovely "Look what I made!" feeling. More people are crafting because it's fun, and this book will cater to those who are discovering how rewarding it is to make your own stuff, without any sort of sewing involved.

And hey, even if you have a sewing machine, maybe it's a pain to pull out. Or you're just plain tired of using it. Maybe it has some setting issues that cause frustrated hair pulling. Grrr . . . I have *so* been there! So, leave that machine in its storage case, gather a few universal tools, and let me show you how easy it is to make commonly sewn items sans a sewing machine.

Oh, and be prepared for a few impressed looks when you reveal that the new curtain/scarf/pillow you assembled was indeed made by your own two little hands. And then revel in the look of surprise when you confess that not one single stitch was involved. Gratifying indeed!

Just do me one favor. There are projects that cater to different skill levels in this book. Start with the easy ones at first, if need be, but promise me that you won't limit yourself to the simplest just because you don't consider yourself very skilled at crafting. One of my favorite feelings is the delight that comes from trying something that I feel intimidated by and then shocking my own socks right off when I see the results. No joke: it's like a natural drug . . . and you'll love it! Do we have a deal? Good.

Now, go and have some fun, share your projects with me, and beautify the people and living spaces around you!

–Ashley

Getting Started

SUPPLY LIST

Many of the projects within this book require the same tools. Instead of listing each of the common (and sometimes basic household) items for every single project, I've put together a master list here, broken down into three categories. Items listed under The Basics below will be included in a "Toolkit" list for each project, because I figure you're likely to have them on hand already. I've also included the types and brands of some of my favorite supplies, which may help you in deciding what to select. You don't have to purchase (or have on hand) every single item listed to begin working on projects, but just keep in mind that the following tools are used fairly often throughout the book.

The Basics

- RULER
  You may want several types. My favorites to have on hand are a clear ruler (helps to see what's going on underneath), a short hem guide ruler (with a slide that adjusts for your desired folded amount of fabric), and a standard 12-inch ruler.

- FLEXIBLE MEASURING TAPE
  Flexible measuring tape, often made out of vinyl, is used to measure three-dimensional objects such as a waist, arms, etc.

- FABRIC SCISSORS
  It's always best to keep a pair of scissors dedicated to fabric only. This will keep them sharp and will help keep your cutting accurate.

- PAPER SCISSORS
  You will need to cut paper at times, so make sure you have a second pair of scissors, separate from the fabric scissors.

- STRAIGHT PINS

- SAFETY PINS

- CLOTHESPINS

- IRON/IRONING BOARD
  An iron with a steam setting is necessary for the optimal outcome when using fusible adhesive.

- PEN

- PENCIL

- PERMANENT MARKER

- TAILOR'S CHALK
  This type of chalk has a fine tip for accurately marking fabric but erases easily.

- PINKING SHEARS
  The blades of pinking shears are sawtoothed, which cuts the fabric in a zigzag pattern. When you cut woven fabric on the diagonal, it minimizes fraying tremendously.

- LIGHTER
  This will be used to melt ribbon ends. Some may prefer to use a lit candle so that the flame is constant. Just be cautious while working with either option.

- UTILITY KNIFE

- CUTTING MAT

- HAMMER

- MASKING TAPE

The Adhesives

- EPOXY GLUE
  My favorite brand is Amazing Goop Craft. It's permanent, waterproof, and paintable.

- HOT GLUE GUN AND GLUE STICKS
  I have used many glue guns, and I don't necessarily feel that one brand is better than another. However, I strongly encourage buying one that has two heat options. Glue sticks that aren't heated up fully are sometimes useless and don't fully bond to the surface you're working with.

- DOUBLE-SIDED FUSIBLE ADHESIVE TAPE, ½-INCH AND ¼-INCH WIDTHS
  I have tried many, many brands and my absolute favorite, hands-down, is

Steam-A-Seam 2 Double Stick Fusible Web Tape. It's slightly sticky, which helps it temporarily stay in place until you're ready to iron it permanently in place. I use these widths pretty often and like having them both on hand. I have found this brand to be available in many fabric stores and several places online. Always follow the package instructions for use.

- FUSIBLE ADHESIVE SHEETS
  The brand I prefer and use the most is Thermoweb Heat'n Bond iron-on adhesive. It comes in rolls and lasts a long time. Always follow the package instructions for use.

Other Specialty Supplies

- FREEZER PAPER
  This stuff was designed to wrap around meat before placing it in the freezer. However, crafters discovered its usefulness when they figured out that it would iron temporarily to fabric, creating precise templates and pattern pieces. One side is paper, while the other has a glossy finish and adheres quickly to fabric with the use of a heated iron. Freezer paper is generally found in the grocery store, near the foil, plastic wrap, and wax paper.

- GROSGRAIN RIBBON
  This type of ribbon is stiffer and holds its shape better than other ribbon varieties. It has little ribbed lines that run across the ribbon. I reach for it more often than not simply because it's a little more heavy duty than most other ribbon options. However, other satin types of fabric are great for aesthetics, if desired.

- SNAP HAMMER TOOL
  This is my preferred tool for attaching snaps. It's a long metal shaft that has a round end that fits over one side of the snap pieces. You hit the hammer at the top of the shaft, and the round end helps compress your two snap pieces together. (It is shown in all the pictures where a snap tool is needed.)

- SNAP PLIERS
  If you can't locate a snap hammer tool, there are also snap pliers available. I find

them to be a little finicky unless you're willing to invest in a more expensive pair, but they're a fine option.

- EYELET SETTER HAMMER TOOL
  There are several tools available for setting eyelets, but my preferred tool (and most economical) is the basic tool that comes with many packages of eyelet sets. It's a long metal shaft that has a round end that fits over one side of the eyelet pieces. You hit the hammer at the top of the shaft, and the round end helps compress your two eyelet pieces together. (It is shown in all the pictures where an eyelet tool is needed.)

- VINYL (A.K.A. FAUX LEATHER)
  Vinyl is a less expensive choice for projects and behaves similarly to leather but is man-made and a little less breathable. However, it comes in a larger variety of colors and is fade resistant.

- WAISTBAND ELASTIC
  This type of elastic is made in a variety of widths and is most often manufactured as the following types: woven, braided, non-roll, and knit. Though this elastic is typically used inside of waistband casings because of its sturdy construction, it can be used for a variety of other projects as well.

- FOLD-OVER ELASTIC
  This type of elastic is really soft and was initially used as the stretchy waistband

and leg holes of underwear and bloomers. It is now being put to good use in a variety of crafting projects.

- FABRIC PAINT
- DECOUPAGE SEALER
  Decoupage sealer is a glue, sealant, and varnish, all in one. It works as an adhesive but is also great to apply over things to give them a nice sealed finish. My favorite brand is Mod Podge, and matte is the variety I use the most and for many surface types.
- POLYESTER FIBERFILL
- STAPLE GUN
- POWER DRILL

FABRIC GUIDE

Woven Fabric

When a fabric is woven, its fibers are interlaced in a crisscross pattern, horizontally and vertically. Think of weaving strips of paper together in grade school, when you'd interlace the paper to create one big woven swath of paper. Woven fabric is the same way. When cut, the fibers release and start to unravel, causing fraying along the edges. However, because of the weaving method, woven fabric tends to hold its shape better and doesn't really stretch. This can be helpful when trying to keep things precise and perfectly even and straight.

Cutting along the grain of the fabric means cutting parallel to the woven fibers that create woven fabric.

One way to slow down the fraying of woven fabric is to cut on the "bias." This means that you are cutting at a diagonal (45-degree angle) across the interlaced horizontal and vertical fibers. The bias of woven fabric also has some stretch to it and will hang differently than fabric that has been cut along the grain.

Knit Fabric

When a fabric is knit, there is one continuous thread being looped together back and forth. Upon close inspection, the pattern almost looks like braiding. Because of that loopy, braided technique, the fabric has a lot more give and stretch. Knit fabric is a great friend to the crafter because once cut, its edges don't fray like wovens do, since it's only one continuous thread rather than many separate  threads. Depending on the type of knit fabric, the edges may curl a bit once they're cut, but if the curled edge doesn't affect the look of the project much, it doesn't really matter.

Remember, it's the method, not the type of fiber, that distinguishes whether a fabric is woven or knit. Cotton, rayon, wool, polyester, and silk can all be woven or knit.

IDENTIFYING WOVEN/KNIT FABRIC: Grab your fabric and stretch it from side to side and from top to bottom, in the same direction as the grain. If it stretches in one of those directions (or both), it is probably a knit. If it doesn't stretch with the grain and only stretches very slightly when pulled diagonally on the bias, it's most likely a woven. The only time a woven fabric will stretch with the grain is if elastic fibers are woven into the fabric.

SYNTHETIC FABRIC (NYLON, POLYESTER, RAYON): Synthetic fabric is quite sensitive to heat. Steer clear of using synthetic fabric while constructing items from this book. The fibers are more prone to melting and won't be able to withstand the excessive ironing and steaming necessary to activate the fusible adhesive used frequently throughout the book.

"RIGHT" AND "WRONG" SIDES OF FABRIC: Most fabrics have designated sides that are meant to be "seen" and "not seen." Each side will likely have a different color or texture, or both. If your fabric has a design printed onto it, you will notice that the "right" ("seen") side is more vibrant. Sometimes it's hard to tell the difference between the sides, and if that's the case, it won't likely matter which side you choose as the "right" side.

Helpful Tips

Read this section in its entirety before starting any project!

When using fusible adhesive tape to fuse fabric layers together, don't get frustrated if you don't achieve a strong adhesion right away. It will take some time to figure out how your adhesive reacts with your iron and fabric. Always check your iron heat first and turn it up a bit and see if that helps. If not, try adding a little bit of steam to help heat up and moisten the adhesive, creating an even stronger bond. After a few seconds of consistent heat, lift up your iron, check your bond, and repeat if necessary. Just be sure to hold consistent heat on your fabric long enough for a good seal.

Sometimes when using thicker fabric, your adhesive may have a hard time holding everything in place. You'll want to first increase the time that you hold the iron on the fabric and then check the fusion. However, you may want to consider adding two or three layers of your fusible adhesive tape in place of a single layer, and then try ironing again. When ironing fusible tape or sheets, never pull the iron across the fabric. Always press down your iron, lift up, move locations, and press down again.

Using hot glue can be a little messy. Before using hot glue on any project, practice making even lines and then lifting, without dragging away long strings of glue. To eliminate strings, it helps to release the glue, then let go of the trigger while still holding the tip over the extracted glue. Then move the tip over the hot glue area until most of the excess comes out of the tip of the gun, and pull away quickly. This will take some practice, but it's worth getting the method down so you don't spoil a project with messy blobs of glue.

If you do see blobs of dried hot glue that have turned white, don't give up just yet. Use a lighter to heat up the glue and try wiping it away quickly with your finger (careful—it will be hot). If it's only a small bit that you're trying to remove, you may not even need to wipe it away. But heating it up will turn it clear again, making it fairly unnoticeable.

All items created with fusible adhesive are considered a little more sensitive to harsh cleaning methods. Clothing made with fusible adhesive should be washed on a gentle cycle (or hand washed, if you're extra concerned) and then placed flat to air-dry. You will also need to iron your fabric and check any of your fusible adhesives for lifting (which can be remedied with re-ironing). Consider clothing items made with fusible adhesive more like specialty items in your wardrobe, not "everyday" clothing that can withstand regular wear and tear. It's certainly worth having a few handmade pieces for a special occasion or season, even if you have to take a little more time caring for them.

When ironing fusible adhesives, be sure that they don't come in direct contact with the iron. They should be sandwiched between the two layers of fabric and not poking out anywhere. If adhesive gets on your iron, it can be transferred to other parts of your project and could ruin your hard work. If you do happen to get some adhesive on the face of your iron, try carefully rubbing it off with a hand towel while the iron is still on and hot. There are also iron cleaners available at most fabric stores.

Never place your iron over an area that has previously been glued. The heated glue will become sticky again and will not only make a mess of your iron/work surface, but will loosen up the adhesion and may ruin the placement of your fabrics.

Cutting a straight line in your fabric can be tricky. Make it easier by using a ruler to draw a straight line onto your fabric with tailor's chalk and then cut along the line. Another method is to line up the fabric along a table or counter edge and use that as a guide. A method that works for some woven fabrics is to pull one of the horizontal or vertical fibers, creating a puckered line in the fabric. Continue to tug until you've pulled the fiber all the way out. Use the line made by the missing fiber as your straight line and cut along it.

The time estimate listed for each project is just that: an estimate. It can vary from one skill level to another and can also be affected by the types of supplies used.

If you are making clothing items for someone other than yourself or someone you can measure, use these woman and child sizing charts for reference. (Remember, every body size is a little different and won't fit exactly according to this chart. However, for the purposes of the clothing projects in this book, estimates will do when necessary.)

Women's Sizing Chart

size	XS (0–2)	S (4–6)	M (8–10)	L (12–14)	XL (16)	XXL (18)
waist	24.5–25.5	26.5–27.5	28.5–29.5	31–32.5	34	36
hips	33.5–34.5	35–36	37–38	39–41	42–44	46

All measurements are in inches.

Measurements are standard sizes from a general population. The most accurate measurement is to measure your actual subject.

Children's Sizing Chart

age	6 mos.	12 mos.	2	3	4	5	6	8	10	12
height	24–26.5	28.5–30.5	33–35	36–38	39–42	42–44	44–47	49–52	53–56	58–62
chest	19	20	21	22	23	24	25	27	29	31
waist	19	19.5	20	20.75	21.5	22.5	23.5	25	26	27
neck circ.	8.5	9	9.5	10	11	11.5	12	13	13.5	14

All measurements are in inches.

Measurements are standard sizes from a general population. The most accurate measurement is to measure your actual subject.

Resource Guide

A few places to consider while shopping for your supplies:

- Jo-Ann Fabric
- Hobby Lobby
- Hancock Fabrics
- Local fabric shops in your area
- fabric.com
- chezami.com (a great site for knit fabrics, in particular)
- girlcharlee.com (a great site for knit fabrics)
- amazon.com
- createforless.com
- etsy.com

Chapter 1

HOME DÉCOR

GROMMET CURTAIN PANEL

Luckily, something as easy as switching out curtain panels can really change the look of a room that you're growing tired of. Making your own curtains gives you the freedom to make them the exact size, shape, color, and thickness that you need. And grommets are a simple concept that will really make your curtains pop!

SKILL LEVEL: II   »   TIME ESTIMATE: 60–90 MINUTES

Supplies

- Medium-weight upholstery fabric, 55–60 inches wide (amount depends on curtain sizes needed)
- Double-sided fusible adhesive tape, ½ inch wide
- 1½-inch curtain grommets
- Curtain rod, less than 1½ inches in diameter (slide grommets onto rod before assembling to check the fit)

Toolkit

- Scissors
- Measuring tape
- Hem guide ruler
- Pen or fine-tip marker
- Iron/ironing board

You'll need about six grommets for each 55- to 60-inch-wide curtain panel.

1. Determine the curtain height that you need and add 7½ inches to that measurement. If you're making one panel per window, measure the width of your window and multiply by 1½. That will be your fabric width dimension. If you're making two panels per window, measure the width of your window and divide by 2. Then multiply that number by 1½ and that will be your fabric width dimension for each of the two panels. (If you want fuller curtains, multiply your measurements by 2 instead of 1½.) Add 2 inches to the width of each panel, for finishing your side edges. Cut the fabric to these dimensions. Fold one of your side edges over ½ inch, with the wrong sides together, and iron flat.

2. Fold it over another ½ inch and iron again.

3. Lift the folded edge up and place a strip of fusible adhesive tape in the fold, the whole length of the curtain.

4. Fold the flap of fabric back down and iron it in place according to the adhesive's package instructions. Avoid pulling or dragging the iron across the fabric.

5. Repeat with the other side edge of your curtain panel.

6. Fold the top edge of your curtain over ½ inch, wrong sides together, and iron flat.

7. Fold it over another 4½ inches and iron again.

8. Lift the folded edge up and place a strip of fusible adhesive tape in the fold, the whole width of the curtain. Fold the flap of fabric back down and iron it in place.

9. You will see a gap in each of the sides of the panel where you folded over the top edge of your fabric. Open up each gap and place a piece of adhesive inside. Iron flat, fusing those layers together.

10. Situate the curtain in front of you with the right side facing down and determine where you'd like to place each grommet along the top of the panel. Mark the center of each with a dot. Be sure that you are centering each dot from top to bottom of the folded over 4½-inch-wide section. Mark the grommet closest to each end about 2 inches from the edge. The rest of the grommet dots should be evenly spaced between them.

11. Read the grommet package instructions and follow the directions for drawing templates for each grommet, centering your template on each of the dots that you marked along the top of your curtain panel.

12. Cut out the holes for each grommet.

Follow the instructions for placing the front and back grommet pieces.

Then snap them together.

13. Fold the bottom edge up ½ inch, wrong sides together, and iron it flat. Fold it over another 2 inches and iron it again. Add the fusible adhesive tape under the folded flap of fabric, the entire width of the curtain, and iron it in place.

14. Thread the curtain rod through the grommets, and hang.

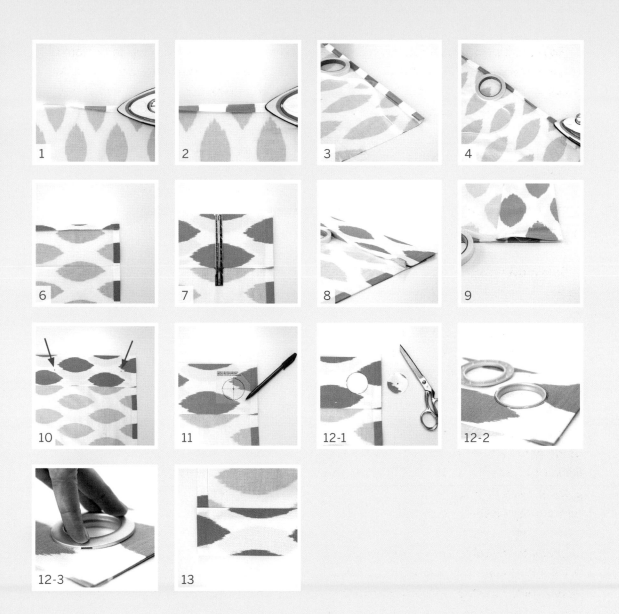

Tips!

If you need curtains that are wider than the piece of fabric you're working with, you'll have to fuse pieces of fabric together to create a wider piece (see the Valentine Tablecloth, page 170). However, if your curtains are mostly for decoration, you can just keep them pulled open and it won't matter that they aren't technically wide enough to cover your window. No one will ever know!

REVERSIBLE TABLE RUNNER

A table runner makes such a pretty addition to table settings, especially when you get to make it the exact color, length, and width that you want. And in case you have a fickle personality, this reversible runner will allow you to change your mind and switch up your look any time you want.

SKILL LEVEL: II » TIME ESTIMATE: 60–90 MINUTES

Supplies

- 1½ yards top fabric, medium-weight cotton
- 1½ yards bottom fabric, medium-weight cotton
- Double-sided fusible adhesive tape, ½ inch wide

Toolkit

- Scissors
- Pinking shears
- Measuring tape
- Ruler or hem guide ruler
- Straight pins
- Iron/ironing board

The finished table runner measures 14 x 102 inches. If you prefer a shorter or longer runner, adjust accordingly.

1. Cut your top fabric into two 15 x 54-inch pieces. Place the pieces end to end, with the right sides facing up. Overlap the two ends, folding the top piece under ½ inch and pressing with an iron. Shift it around a bit to match up any sort of print (if applicable). Just be sure not to overlap them too much, to where the entire length is less than 103 inches (or your table runner will be shorter than the intended 102-inch length). Once you have a good placement, pin the folded end down onto the other piece of fabric.

2. Lift the top fold carefully, removing one pin at a time, and place a strip of fusible adhesive tape along the underside.

3. Iron it in place according to the adhesive's package instructions, fusing the layers together. Avoid pulling or dragging the iron across the fabric.

4. Flip the runner over and trim the extra fabric along the fold down to an inch.

5. Trim the edge again very minimally, using pinking shears this time, to eliminate any fraying of the raw edges. Repeat the cutting and fusing steps with the coordinating bottom fabric.

6. Line up the top and bottom fabrics with the right sides together. Match up the sides and ends and pin in place. Unpin the fabric at one of the short ends and fold the top layer of fabric back a few inches. Place fusible adhesive tape on the bottom layer of fabric, along the very edge of the right side of the fabric. Place the top fabric back on top, match up the edges again, and iron it in place, fusing the right sides together.

7. Continue down the length of the table runner, fusing the top and bottom fabrics together along both long edges, working with about 15 inches or so at a time.

8. Once you reach the second short end, place fusible adhesive tape around the remaining edges and along the end, leaving a 10-inch gap without any adhesive between the two corners (which will be used for turning it right side out). (Use the arrows in photo 8 as a guide for placement.)

Fuse the remaining edges together with your iron, making sure that your gap was left unfused.

9. Trim off all four corners, carefully feeling where your adhesive is placed between the layers of fabric. You are just taking away some bulk in the corners before turning it right side out so that your corners will lie flat. Don't cut too much away, or you'll have a hole when you turn your corner right side out.

10. Turn the table runner right side out through the unfused opening, poking each corner out gently with the closed tip of your scissors. (Don't poke too hard or you'll create a hole.) Fold the edges of the opening toward the inside ½ inch and iron flat. Iron the rest of the table runner flat as well.

11. Place a strip of fusible adhesive tape along the inside edge of the opening, between the top and bottom fabric layers. Place the tape as close as you can to the folded edges of the fabric but hidden enough so that it won't show from the outside. Iron until sealed completely shut.

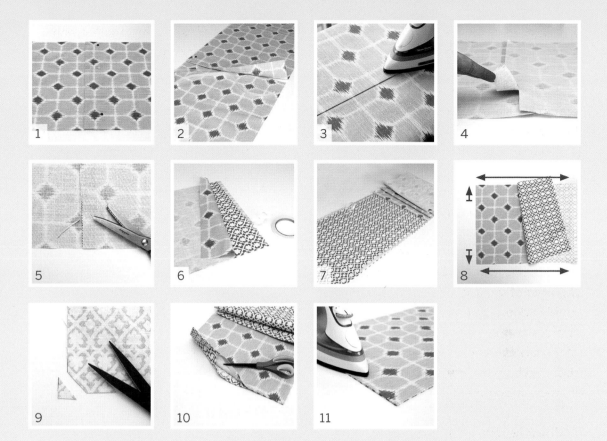

Tips!

If you'd rather purchase more fabric so that you don't have to piece your fabric together (and have to match up patterns, etc.), purchase 3 yards of each type of fabric and cut each top and bottom strip into 15 x 103-inch pieces. Then start with step 6. (You'll have enough fabric left over to keep for other projects or for another identical table runner to give to a friend.)

RUFFLED PILLOW COVER

Ruffles add a fun texture to things, especially a pillow. This ruffled pillow cover has a simple design, with several rows of pre-ruffled trim added right to the front. The back has an envelope closure, so your pillow insert can easily be removed for cleaning.

SKILL LEVEL: III » TIME ESTIMATE: 60 MINUTES

Supplies

- 1 yard cotton fabric, printed or solid (any fabric weight)
- 4 yards pre-ruffled trim, 1¼ inches wide (if you use something narrower or wider, you'll have to adjust the amount of trim needed)
- Double-sided fusible adhesive tape, ½ inch wide
- 16-inch square pillow form

Toolkit

- Scissors
- Measuring tape
- Ruler or hem guide ruler
- Straight pins
- Iron/ironing board

1. Cut out a front piece of fabric that is 17 x 17 inches and two back pieces that are each 12 x 17 inches (these pieces will create the envelope closure).

2. Place one of your back pieces right side down in front of you. Then fold over one of the long edges ½ inch and iron it flat. Then fold it over another ½ inch and iron again. This will be the top of the pillow back. Do the same thing on one long edge of the other back piece. This will be the bottom of the pillow back. (If you're using solid fabric, you won't necessarily need to orient the fabric in any particular way. But if you're using patterned fabric, be sure that the fabric for the top and bottom pieces is facing the same direction.)

3. With the right sides of your back pieces still facing down, lift up one of the narrow flaps that you just ironed down and place a strip of fusible adhesive tape underneath, the entire length of the long edge. Then fold the flap back down and iron it

according to the adhesive's package instructions, fusing the layers together. Avoid pulling or dragging the iron across the fabric. Repeat with the other back piece of fabric.

4. Place both back pieces of fabric right side up and overlap the two folded edges to form a 17 x 17-inch square.

5. Lift apart the overlapping edges and place a strip of fusible adhesive tape between the two layers where they overlap, along the outer edges. You should have about 5 inches of overlapping fabric on the pillow back on each side. Before you iron the tape, measure your pillow back to be sure it is still 17 x 17 inches. Iron together, then repeat on the opposite side.

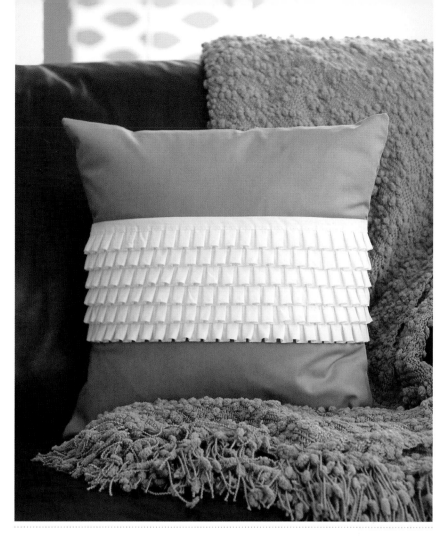

6. Begin cutting strips of your ruffled trim, 17 inches wide.

7. The trim likely has one edge that is raw, or needs to be hidden in the finished project. Lay your front fabric piece right side up and determine where the trim pieces will be placed on the fabric. Use pins to mark where the top row of ruffle trim will start and where the last row will end.

8. Start with the very bottom row of ruffled trim. Place a strip of fusible adhesive tape under the raw edge of the trim and iron it flat to adhere the strip to the pillow front. Be sure to only iron along the top flat edge of the trim, so as not to flatten the ruffles.

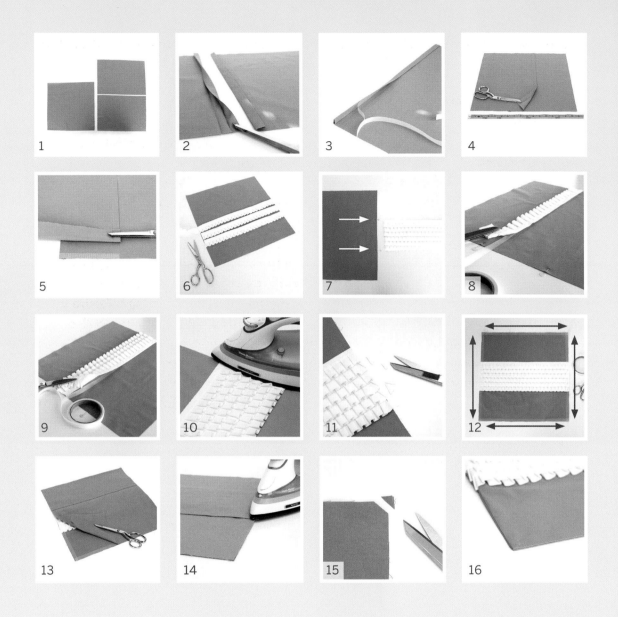

9. Continue adding the rows of trim, one at a time, until all are adhered to the pillow front.

10. In order to join the pillow front and back pieces together, you'll need to flatten the edges of the pillow front, where the rows of ruffles end. Place your iron along the sides of the pillow, ironing the edges of the ruffles flat, about ½ inch inward.

11. Trim any overhanging trim as needed, keeping the 17-inch square.

12. Place strips of fusible adhesive tape around all the edges of the pillow front, keeping it exactly even with all four outer edges and overlapping at each corner. (Use the arrows on photo 12 as a guide for placement.)

13. Place the pillow back on top, facedown, making the opening of the pillow back parallel with the rows of ruffles, rather than perpendicular.

14. Iron around all four edges of the pillow, activating all of the adhesive strips.

15. Trim off the excess fabric from each corner (about ¼ inch) to remove some of the bulk. Make sure not to cut all the way through the adhesive at each corner, however, or you'll have a hole in your corner after turning it right side out.

16. Turn the pillow cover right side out through the back opening. Gently poke out each corner and then iron along each edge, making sure that none of the adhesive is exposed. If a bit of the adhesive pulled loose while you were turning the cover right side out, iron it again and it will re-adhere without any problem. Then stuff your insert (or old pillow) inside the cover.

Tips!

A variety of fabric weights work well for this project. A thicker fabric is a little sturdier and holds its shape better but may need a double layer of adhesive strips to keep the fabric layers together (see Helpful Tips, page 13). However, a lighter-weight fabric offers a softer texture and a slightly different look to your pillow. Go with what suits you best.

A knitting needle or the point of your closed scissors can be helpful in poking out your pillow corners. Be sure to do so gently so you don't poke a hole through the fabric.

FABRIC PLACEMAT

Need a perfect housewarming, wedding, or welcome-to-the-neighborhood gift? Or just want a particular placemat color to match your dining room setting? No more searching every store in town for the perfect color or print: just make your own!

SKILL LEVEL: I » TIME ESTIMATE: 60 MINUTES

Supplies

- ½ yard outer fabric (medium- to heavy-weight fabrics work best)
- ½ yard lining fabric (medium- to heavy-weight fabrics work best)
- Double-sided fusible adhesive tape, ½ inch wide

Toolkit

- Scissors
- Measuring tape
- Iron/ironing board

Supplies listed are to complete one 14 x 18-inch placemat.

1. Cut a 15 x 19-inch rectangle from each fabric.

2. Place some fusible adhesive tape along the edges of your outer fabric piece, on the right side of the fabric. Overlap the tape at each corner, making sure that all edges have adhesive. Leave an 8-inch gap in the adhesive along one side (for turning right side out later on), centering the gap between the two corners. (Use the arrows in photo 2 as a guide for placement.)

3. Place your lining fabric right side down directly on top of the outer fabric, matching up all edges. Be sure that the fusible adhesive tape hasn't moved and is still lined up with the outer edges of both layers of fabric.

4. Iron your layers together according to the adhesive's package instructions. Avoid pulling or dragging the iron across the fabric. All edges should fuse together, except for the gap along the side.

5. Trim off the excess fabric at all four corners, carefully feeling where your adhesive is between the layers of fabric, so as not to cut through the adhesive. You are just taking away some bulk here before turning it right side out so that your corners will lie flat. Don't cut too much, or you'll have a hole when you turn your corner right side out.

6. Turn the placemat right side out through the opening on one side, poking each corner out gently with the closed tip of your scissors. (Don't poke too hard or you'll create a hole.) Fold the edges of the opening toward the inside ½ inch and iron flat. Iron the rest of the placemat flat as well.

7. Place a strip of fusible adhesive tape along the inside edge of the opening, between the fabric layers. Place the tape as close as you can to the folded edges of the fabric but hidden enough so that it won't show from the outside. Iron until sealed completely shut.

Tips!

The supply list calls for ½ yard of each of your fabrics to make one placemat. That's because you need at least ½ yard for the height dimension of the placemat. However, fabric is usually 44–45 inches wide, and sometimes up to 60. So, you can absolutely cut two placemats from the fabrics needed to make the one placemat.

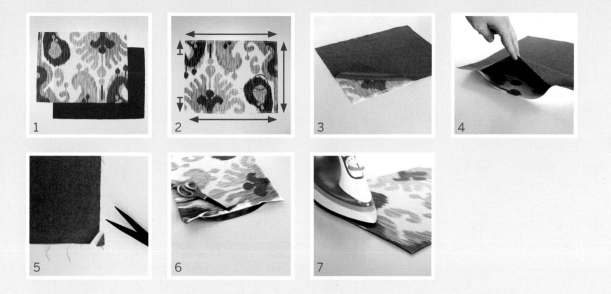

BASKET LINER

Adding a liner to a basket has multiple purposes. The liner helps keep the wicker fibers clean and also helps keep the basket's contents from being snagged by the wicker's jagged ends. And let's not forget that a little splash of color can really perk up a sad ol' basket!

SKILL LEVEL: I » TIME ESTIMATE: 90 MINUTES

Supplies

- Square/rectangular basket, any size
- Laminated cotton fabric (amount depends on basket size)
- 8 (¼-inch) metal eyelet sets
- Eyelet setter hammer tool (or other eyelet tool)
- Grosgrain ribbon, ⅜ inch wide

Toolkit

- Scissors
- Flexible measuring tape
- Scratch paper
- Scotch tape
- Pen or fine-tip marker
- Hammer

1. To measure the size of fabric needed for your lining, leave a 4-inch overhang of flexible measuring tape over the top edge of the basket, then let your measuring tape drop to the inside of the basket.

2. Pull the tape taut against the inside edge to the bottom of the basket, pull it across the bottom, up the opposite side, and then over, leaving a 4-inch overhang on that side as well. This is your length measurement. Do the same thing in the other direction to get the width, making sure to include the 4-inch overhang on both sides. These will be the dimensions for your fabric.

3. Place your measuring tape flat against the bottom of the basket and measure just the length of the bottom. Then measure the other direction for the width of the bottom.

4. Cut a piece of laminated cotton fabric to fit the dimensions from step 2, and lay it down in front of you, right side up. Then cut a piece of paper the size of the basket base from step 3. Center the paper on top of the laminated fabric and tape it in place. Double-check your placement by measuring the overhang of fabric on all sides.

5. Cut rectangular pieces out of each corner of your fabric, creating a cross shape out of the laminated fabric. Make sure that the width of each end of the cross shape stays consistent with the measurement of its corresponding side of the paper template. Remove the tape and paper.

6. Place the fabric right side up inside of the basket, making sure to orient it to cover the whole bottom of the basket and hang over each side by 4 inches. (If it doesn't fit perfectly, trim it and try again.) Mark a dot in the corner of each flap, where you will place the eyelets, at least a ½ inch away from the edge.

7. For each eyelet that you attach, you will need an eyelet front (taller barrel, *a*), an eyelet back (shorter barrel, *b*), a hammer plate (*c*), and a hammer post (*d*).

8. Center an eyelet back over the dot you drew on one of the flaps and use it as a template to trace around the inside edge of the barrel.

9. Cut out the circle with scissors.

10. Turn the fabric over so that the wrong side is facing up. Place the eyelet front through the hole from the right side, forcing the barrel to poke up through to the wrong side of the fabric. Place the eyelet back on top.

11. Put the hammer plate at the base, underneath the eyelet front, and then fit the hammer post on top of the eyelet back.

12. Tap the top of the hammer post with a regular hammer a few times, until both eyelet pieces fit together around the fabric nice and tight. Repeat with the other seven eyelets, placing one in each corner of the overhanging flaps.

13. Place the liner back into the basket, fold out each flap evenly, and secure the flaps in pairs at each corner with a piece of ribbon.

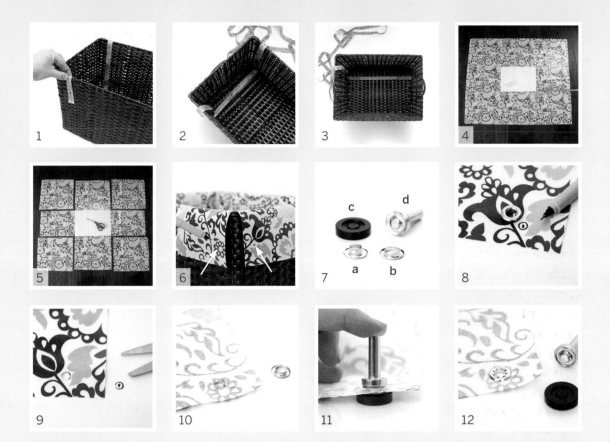

Tips!

Laminated fabric is cool stuff! It is coated with a clear vinyl, keeping it from fraying once it's cut. However, you don't want to iron this fabric, or the coating will melt. (If you have a stubborn wrinkle, try using a hairdryer to loosen up the crease. But generally, wrinkles will fall out once the fabric is fitted into the basket.)

Laminated fabric is becoming more common in local stores, but there is a larger variety found online. You can also create your own laminated fabric by purchasing iron-on clear vinyl and fusing it right over the top of your fabric, according to the package instructions.

If you'd like more or less of a lining overhang on the outside of the basket, adjust the 4-inch measurement accordingly.

PIPED PILLOW COVER

Who says you can only attach piping with a sewing machine? Ignore the naysayers and create a beautifully trimmed pillow cover, stuff it with a cozy pillow insert, and then toss it onto your sofa, bench seat, or bed. Now admire your gorgeous little pop of color!

SKILL LEVEL: III » **TIME ESTIMATE: 90 MINUTES**

Supplies

- 1 yard medium- or heavy-weight home décor cotton fabric
- Double-sided fusible adhesive tape, ½ inch wide
- 1 (3-yard) package coordinating piping
- 18-inch square pillow form

Toolkit

- Scissors
- Measuring tape
- Clear ruler or measuring tape
- Straight pins
- Iron/ironing board

1. Cut out a front piece from your fabric that is 19 x 19 inches and two back pieces that are 13 x 19 inches.

2. Place one of your back pieces right side down in front of you, long edges parallel to your work surface. Then fold over the top long edge ½ inch and iron it flat. Fold it over another ½ inch and iron again. Do the same thing to the bottom long edge of the other back piece. (If you're using printed fabric, be sure to match up the pattern so that it goes in the same direction on both pieces. For solid fabrics, you won't necessarily have a "top" or "bottom.")

3. Lift up one of the narrow flaps that you just ironed down and place a strip of fusible adhesive tape underneath, along the entire length of the edge. Then fold the flap back down and iron it according to the adhesive's package instructions. Avoid pulling or dragging the iron across the fabric. Repeat with the other back piece of fabric.

4. Place both back pieces of fabric right-side up and overlap the two folded edges to form a 19 x 19 square. Then pin the two sides together along the overlapping raw edges.

5. Remove the pins on one side without moving the fabric and then fold up the edge of the top layer just a bit. Place a strip of fusible adhesive tape between the raw edges of the two layers. Be sure to line up the tape exactly on the edge of the bottom fabric first and then the edge of the top layer. Measure to be sure that this side is still 19 inches wide. Iron it flat to activate the adhesive. Repeat on the opposite side, where the edges overlap as well. You now have a front and back piece that are both 19 x 19 inches.

6. Fold a length of fusible adhesive tape in half longways and begin pinning it to the bottom edge of the piping. (Folding it in half will help the adhesive fit better, but it also adds a double layer of adhesive to the piping.) You will notice that there's a seam right below the bump of the piping. Line the top edge of the folded fusible adhesive tape right along that seam so that it doesn't hang below the bottom edge. Pin the adhesive to the piping every couple of inches.

7. Lay your pillow front down in front of you, right side up. (And if applicable, make sure your print is right side up as well.) Starting at the bottom center, begin pinning the piping to the fabric with the adhesive facing down, and with the seam of the piping ½ inch from the bottom raw edge of the pillow fabric. Let the very end of the piping gradually curve off the fabric and pin it in place.

8. Once you reach the corner, make a cut in the bottom half of the piping (right up to the seam but not through it) ½ inch from the right edge of the fabric. This will help your piping turn the corner.

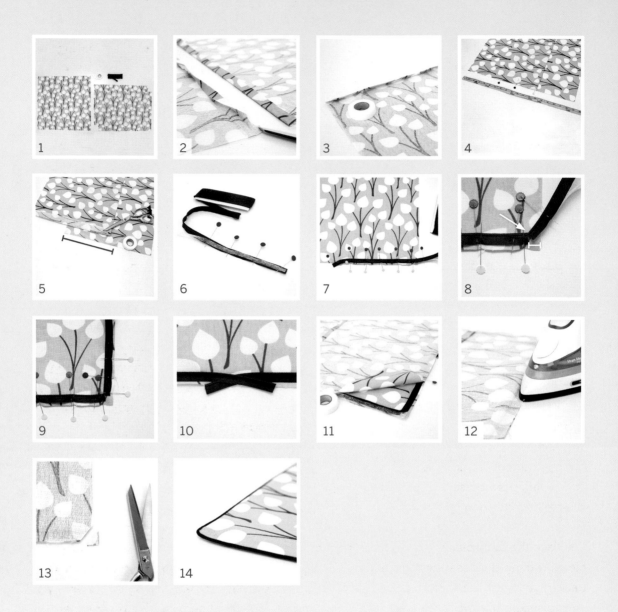

1

2

3

4

5

6

7

8

9

10

11

12

13

14

Tips!

If you already have an 18-inch throw pillow that no longer matches your décor (or has become worn), use that as your insert rather than buying a new one.

9. Be sure to pin the piping to the fabric really close to the corner cut on both the bottom and right sides, to force a nicely squared piped corner. Then continue pinning your piping along the next side of the pillow fabric.

10. Continue all the way around the front pillow piece, keeping everything lined up and ½ inch from the edge. Once you make it all the way around, overlap the ends of the piping, letting the excess piping run off the edge of the fabric. Leave a 1-inch tail on both ends and then iron the piping in place, butting the edge of the iron right up against the bump of the piping. Be sure to lift and press with the iron and remove pins as you go, checking to see that the adhesive has completely melted and has adhered to both the fabric and the piping. If not, keep pressing with the iron. Spend some extra time ironing where the two ends overlap, to be sure that the adhesive has created a strong hold.

11. Place the back piece on top of the front piece, with right sides together, keeping track of your print direction if needed. Use pins to secure the two layers together, all the way around. Then remove the pins from one side and lift up the top fabric edge just a bit in order to place a strip of the fusible adhesive tape between the layers, lining it up right below the bump of the piping.

12. Iron the two layers together, making sure to lift and then place the iron back down rather than pulling it across the fabric, all the way along the side. Repeat with the other three sides. While ironing, butt the iron right up against the edge of the piping, getting the adhesive between the layers nice and hot. Check around all the edges to be sure that the adhesive did its job. (Looking at it from the inside to see if the edges adhered to each other properly is also helpful. If they have not, iron everything again.)

13. Trim each of the four corners off, making sure to not cut through the curve of the piping but right up against it. (Cutting the corners will take away some of the bulk, making a prettier corner after you turn it right side out.)

14. Turn the pillow cover right side out through the back opening. Gently poke out each corner and then iron along each edge, making sure that the fabric is folded right up against the piping. Help it along if necessary. If a bit of the adhesive pulled loose while you were turning the cover right side out, iron it again and it will re-adhere without any problem. Then stuff your insert (or old pillow) inside the cover.

GROCERY BAG HOLDER

Do you have an overflowing stash of plastic grocery bags in your pantry or cupboard that has become unruly? How about creating a fabric holder that neatly stores all of those bags, with a stretchy place to insert them at the top and the ability to easily pull what you need from the bottom? It's a much lovelier solution than just shoving all the bags inside one large plastic bag.

SKILL LEVEL: II » TIME ESTIMATE: 90 MINUTES

Supplies

- ¾ yard medium-weight cotton fabric
- Double-sided fusible adhesive tape, ¼ inch wide and ½ inch wide
- 32 (¼-inch) metal eyelet sets
- Eyelet setter hammer tool (or other eyelet tool)
- 14 inches grosgrain ribbon, ⅝ inch wide
- Epoxy glue
- 1 yard cord elastic, ⅛ inch wide

Toolkit

- Scissors
- Pinking shears
- Measuring tape
- Ruler or hem guide ruler
- Straight pins
- Pen of fine-tip marker
- Iron/ironing board
- Hammer
- Lighter

The finished grocery bag holder is approximately 21 inches tall. When it's stuffed with bags, it's 6–7 inches wide.

1. Cut your fabric into a 24 x 20-inch piece.

2. Fold a short (20-inch) edge over ½ inch, wrong sides together, and iron flat.

3. Fold it over again, but 1 inch this time, and iron flat.

4. Lift the folded edge back up and place a strip of ½-inch-wide fusible adhesive tape along the upper folded edge, all the way across.

5. Fold the flap of fabric back down and iron it in place according to the adhesive's package instructions. Avoid pulling or dragging the iron across the fabric. Repeat with opposite short edge.

6. Fold your fabric in half lengthwise, with right sides together, matching up the two raw edges. Place a piece of ½-inch-wide fusible adhesive tape between the two edges and then iron flat, fusing the fabric layers together.

Trim the very edge of the fused layers with pinking shears, which will keep the edge from fraying.

7. Turn the tube of fabric right side out and iron flat. Make sure to iron the excess flap of fabric down flat on the inside, feeling with your hand as you iron.

Turn the tube inside out again and lift up the excess flap of fabric that you just ironed down in the previous step and place a strip of ¼-inch-wide fusible adhesive tape under the flap.

8. Press the excess fabric flap back down and iron it to activate the adhesive.

9. For each eyelet that you attach, you will need an eyelet front (taller barrel, *a*), an eyelet back (shorter barrel, *b*), a hammer plate (*c*), and a hammer post (*d*).

10. Turn the tube right side out and place sixteen evenly spaced straight pins along the end of your tube, right where each of your sixteen eyelets will be attached. Place an eyelet down about ¼ inch from the top edge of your tube, in line with one of the straight pins. Trace a circle onto the fabric, using the inside barrel of the eyelet as a template.

11. Cut out the circle with some sharp and pointy scissors.

12. Place the eyelet front through the hole from the right side of the fabric, forcing the barrel to poke through to the wrong side of the fabric.

13. Place the right side of the fabric face-down and then slide the hammer plate underneath the eyelet front. Place the eyelet back on top of the eyelet front and then fit the hammer post on top of the eyelet back. Tap the top of the hammer post with a regular hammer a few times, until both eyelet pieces compress and pinch the fabric in between nice and tight.

Continue installing eyelets across this end of the tube, and then repeat across the other end (you'll have thirty-two total eyelets).

14. Use a lighter to slightly melt and seal both ends of your ribbon so they won't fray.

15. Pick one end of your tube to be the "top" end, since they're identical at this point. Thread one end of your ribbon through an eyelet and fold it over onto itself by 1 inch. Add some epoxy glue and pinch closed. Apply pressure and let the glue dry completely.

Insert the other end of ribbon through an eyelet across from the first one and glue the end the same as the first, creating a handle for your holder.

16. Weave a piece of elastic through the eyelets, including the eyelets where the ribbon is looped through. Cinch it just a bit, so that this top end of your bag holder will keep the bags in place but isn't too small to shove bags through with your hand. Then tie the two elastic ends together.

17. Do the same thing at the bottom end of your holder, but cinch the elastic in a little tighter to hold the plastic bags inside. Trim the excess elastic at both ends.

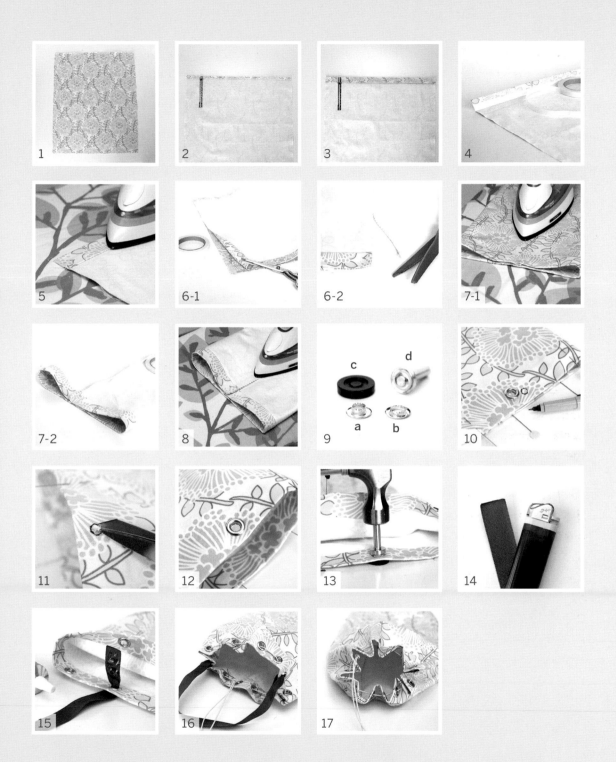

TUFTED HEADBOARD

There's just something beautiful and grand about crowning a mattress with an upholstered headboard. And to then add tufting on top of that? Gorgeous. Customize your own headboard with the fabrics you want and the exact dimensions you need to fit your bedroom perfectly. Relaxing in your room never felt so good!

SKILL LEVEL: III » TIME ESTIMATE: 3–4+ HOURS

Supplies

- Headboard drawing guide (pages 236–237)
- Plywood, ⅝ inch thick
- Saw
- Drill and drill bit (same size as your bolt diameter)
- Foam, 1½ inch thick
- Spray adhesive
- Loft quilt batting, 1 inch thick
- Staple gun/heavy duty staples
- Medium-weight fabric
- Long-neck screwdriver (or awl)
- 1-inch washers (they should fit the bolts)
- 2-inch bolts with matching locknuts
- Nut driver (or ratchet)
- 1 x 4s (wood pieces)
- Backing fabric
- 1½-inch flat-head screws
- 1¼-inch cover button kit
- Epoxy glue

Toolkit

- Scissors
- Measuring tape
- Iron
- Straight pins
- Pencil

	King	Queen	Full	Twin
Plywood	78 x 35 inches	62 x 35 inches	56 x 35 inches	40 x 35 inches
Foam	78 x 35 inches	62 x 35 inches	56 x 35 inches	40 x 35 inches
Batting	Enough to cover plywood surface plus 8 inches on all sides	Enough to cover plywood surface plus 8 inches on all sides	Enough to cover plywood surface plus 8 inches on all sides	Enough to cover plywood surface plus 8 inches on all sides
1 x 4s (8 feet long)	3	3	3	3
Fabric	3½ yards	3 yards	2¾ yards	2½ yards
Cover buttons	30	26	22	18
Washers, bolts, locknuts	30 of each	26 of each	22 of each	18 of each

*The above measurements are based on standard bed sizes. Always measure your bed first to be sure these specifications will work for you.

*A standard bed height is about 25 inches from the top of the mattress down to the floor. Headboards usually rise 25–35 inches above the mattress. The main portion of this headboard is designed to begin right at the top of the mattress and then extend 35 inches upward, while the legs extend 25 inches below the headboard, down to the floor. If these measurements won't work for your bed, make adjustments as needed.

*Batting and foam come in different widths and sizes. The foam can be cut and pieced together, while the batting should be one large piece following the specifications in the chart.

1. Cut your plywood to size and draw your lines and dots onto the plywood following the diagram (page 236–237), according to your headboard size.

2. Situate your plywood off the ground with sturdy objects under each end (paint cans work great) and drill through each dot you have made on your wood. Be sure that the drill bit is the same size as the bolts, so that they slide through easily.

3. Cut your foam down to size to completely cover your piece of plywood. Using smaller pieces of foam and piecing them together is fine, but just keep them nice and snug together.

4. Lift up your foam, one section at a time, and apply spray adhesive to give your foam a temporary hold to the plywood.

5. Place one complete piece of quilt batting over the top of the foam and wrap it around the back of the plywood. Carefully flip the entire thing over (having a second person helps) and pull the batting taut as you staple it to the back side of the plywood, near the edges. Leave about 2 to 3 inches of batting overhang along the back and trim the rest away. (If you'd like an extra layer of cushion, consider adding a second layer of batting in the same way.)

6. Flip the headboard back over to the front and spread your fabric (right side facing up) across your headboard, letting the excess fabric hang evenly around all edges. (Be sure you have enough fabric to wrap around the back of the plywood.) Stick some pins through the fabric and into the foam to hold your fabric in place temporarily.

7. Stand your plywood up on one side and stick a long-neck screwdriver (or awl) through one of the holes in the dead-center of your plywood from the back side. Twist the screwdriver through with one hand while you place pressure on the front side with your other hand, compressing the foam a bit to help the screwdriver cut through the foam and batting.

8. After your screwdriver passes through the foam and batting and reaches the fabric, use your scissors to snip a little hole where the head of the screwdriver meets the fabric.

Push the screwdriver through the hole in the fabric.

9. Slide a washer onto one of your bolts and place the tip of the bolt onto the tip of the screwdriver. Keep firm pressure on the bolt, pushing straight down onto the screwdriver, as you pull the screwdriver back out through the plywood and help the bolt find its way through the layers of foam and batting.

10. Once your bolt has pushed all the way through to the back of the headboard, place a nut on the end and tighten it with a nut driver (or ratchet), while still keeping the foam compressed with your other hand. Your washer on the front will help pull your foam in tight but will also create a nice area for your cover button to sit later on.

11. Repeat this process with the remaining holes on the back of your plywood, working your way outward in a circular pattern (not in a row). Work the fabric into neat tufts between each bolt as you work your way from hole to hole, but don't pull it so tight that you can't easily sink each bolt. Move from hole to hole diagonally, making the tufts stretch in a diamond pattern.

12. Pinch the wrinkles of fabric with your fingers, creating a distinct crease for the tufts. Continually check that you aren't pulling your fabric too far to one side or diagonally;

you want to ensure that there is still enough excess fabric to wrap around the back of your headboard.

13. Once you're finished placing bolts at each hole, turn your headboard facedown onto the paint cans or sturdy risers again. Cut two of your 1 x 4s into equal pieces, which will be mounted on both sides of the headboard. They should each be the length of the height of the headboard plus the desired distance of the headboard from the floor. They will act as legs. Wrap some backing fabric around the bottom part of one of the legs, wrapping it a little higher than where the piece of wood meets the headboard, to be sure no wood is exposed. Staple it in place along the back side of the wood. Fold the fabric around the bottom end of the leg neatly, like you're wrapping a present, and staple in place. Repeat with the other piece of wood.

14. Wrap batting around the upper portion of one of the pieces of wood, covering only to the section that will be attached directly to the back of the plywood. Staple it in place. Repeat with the other piece of wood.

15. Place one of your wood leg pieces flat on the back of the headboard at one side, making sure that the tops, edges, and sides are flush with the headboard. Snip little holes through the batting and then drive your 1½-inch flat-head screws into the wood

pieces, attaching them to the headboard from the back side (two screws at each end). Repeat with the other wood piece along the other side of the headboard.

16. Cut a piece of 1 x 4-inch wood that fits along the very top of the back of the headboard, the whole length of the headboard between the two 1 x 4-inch pieces already mounted. Wrap this piece of wood in batting. Place it at the very top edge of the headboard on the back side, making sure that the top edges are flush with the headboard. Drive 1½-inch screws into both ends and the middle of this piece of wood, the same way you did with the two leg pieces.

17. Pull the fabric from the front of the headboard taut around the edges. Start along the center of the top edge and staple the fabric in place, stapling into the underside of the wood border.

18. Keep the fabric pulled tight and straight as you staple it into place along the back. However, because there will be some excess fabric from all of that tufting along the front side, the fabric won't lie flat and will pucker in places. You'll need to create a little crease above each outside bolt, straight up and over to the back side of the headboard.

19. Staple each little crease in place.

Staple the remaining sides the same way, starting at the middle and working outward, leaving the four corners loose for now. When your sides are done, you'll have some bunched up fabric to deal with at each corner. Start with the upper corners. Fold the excess fabric as neatly as you can, trying to create a nice crisp corner line. (This may take a little manipulating and patience.)

20. Once you get a neat corner, staple it in place.

21. Trim away some of the bulky excess fabric underneath, making sure not to cut away anything that will be seen.

22. Pull the remaining fabric tightly behind the headboard and staple in place.

23. At the two bottom corners, snip the fabric to fit around each leg, tuck under the raw edges, and fold the fabric around the corner of the headboard. Staple in place along the very bottom edge if needed and then pull the excess fabric to the back and staple it out of the way like you did with the upper corners.

24. Flip the headboard over and iron and steam each of the creases.

25. The creases from your tufting will create diamond shapes. Keep the insides of the diamond shapes smooth and flat and each of the creases uniform and crisp.

26. For each bolt that you attached, you'll need a cover button set.

Follow your particular kit instructions and make enough buttons to cover each bolt on your headboard. You should have plenty of fabric after trimming in step 21.

27. If your cover button included a shank on the back, bend that over the best you can so that the button can lie flat on the headboard. Place a generous amount of epoxy glue on the back of the button.

28. Place the glue side down onto the bolt and exposed washer. Be sure that the headboard is lying flat so that the glue doesn't drip while drying. Also, make sure that there's enough glue under there to fill the back of the button and adhere to the bolt and washer, creating a tight seal after the glue dries. However, you don't want too much or it will ooze out around the edges of the button. Press the buttons firmly onto the headboard as they're drying, to ensure that they adhere properly. Let dry completely.

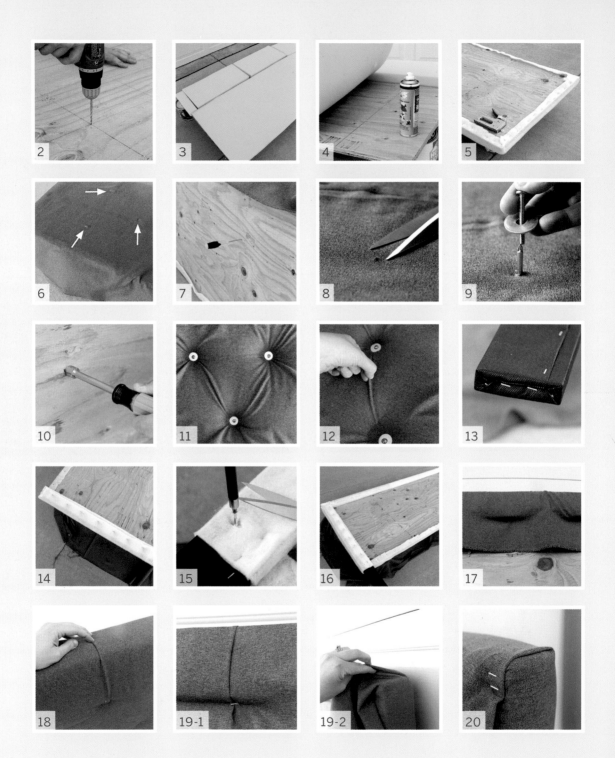

Tips!

If you use thicker or thinner foam, you may need to use longer or shorter bolts for the tufting.

As you're poking all of your holes through the foam with your screwdriver (or awl), it may be easier to lay the headboard down onto the paint cans or risers and reach under as you work, and then place the nuts on temporarily until you can turn the headboard over to really lock them into place. However, do whatever works best for you until you find your rhythm!

The 1 x 4s listed in the supply chart are based on the standard availability of 8-foot long pieces. So, you'll need at least three boards to get the three pieces that you need. However, if you can purchase them in different lengths or have scrap wood at home, determine what's necessary to purchase.

The finished headboard will sit against the wall, and your mattress will sit right beneath the bottom of your headboard. The two headboard legs will be hidden behind the bed and can be bolted to your bed frame for extra security.

LAMP SHADE COVER

Who says you have to keep your plain ol' boring lamp shade? Cover it with some funky fabric and make that little light source pop!

SKILL LEVEL: II » TIME ESTIMATE: 30 MINUTES

Supplies

- Lamp shade (old or new)
- Fabric (amount depends on lamp size)
- Hot glue gun and glue sticks
- Grosgrain ribbon, ⅜ inch wide (enough to go around your lamp shade twice)

Toolkit

- Scissors
- Measuring tape
- Pen or fine-tip marker

1. Lay your lamp shade on the wrong side of your fabric and lightly mark the shape of the shade, rolling it 360 degrees across the fabric to make a complete tracing. Cut out a piece of fabric long enough to go all the way around your lamp shade, leaving an inch of excess at each end and an inch of excess at the top and bottom edges.

2. Hot glue one of the fabric ends (on the wrong side of the fabric) to the lamp shade. Make sure that the lamp shade is centered on the fabric with the inch overhang at the top and bottom of the shade.

3. Wrap the fabric all the way around the shade and fold over the other end of the fabric an inch to hide the cut edge. If the fabric edge won't stay folded, hot glue the fold in place.

4. Pull the fabric taut around the lamp shade and hot glue the folded end to the lamp shade.

5. Fold the top edge down toward the inside of the lamp shade and hot glue it in place. Repeat with the bottom edge.

6. If there is a bar in the way, cut a slit perpendicular to the lamp shade and straight out from the bar.

7. Hot glue ribbon along the top and bottom raw edges of fabric inside the lamp shade in order to hide the edges and also to keep the fabric from fraying any further.

8. Once you make your way around the inside of the lamp shade with your ribbon, stop about 2 inches from the end. Cut off the excess ribbon, leaving enough to fold the ribbon end under an inch and then glue it down, covering the cut end of the ribbon.

Tips!

If your lamp shade is a perfectly shaped cylinder or cube, a striped or geometric pattern will work fine because you can line up the stripes or patterns. However, if you're re-covering an angled lamp shade, it's best to use solid fabric or a print that doesn't have a distinguishable pattern (like a floral).

If you choose a fabric that's too transparent, you'll see the glue lines from the outside, so keep that in mind as you're choosing your fabric.

SIMPLE WINDOW VALANCE

Windows need a little love too, and curtains aren't the only solution. A simple little valance along the top will give that lonely window a splash of color and texture. You'll be amazed at how polished it will make your room look.

SKILL LEVEL: II » TIME ESTIMATE: 60 MINUTES

Supplies

- 2 standard metal curtain rods with curved ends to fit your window, ¾–1 inch wide
- Upholstery fabric (amount depends on valance size you make)
- Double-sided fusible adhesive tape, ½ inch wide

Toolkit

- Scissors
- Flexible measuring tape
- Ruler or hem guide ruler
- Iron/ironing board

1. Mount your top rod to the wall, right above your window. Decide how long you want your valance to hang and then mount your second curtain rod that distance down from the first one. Be sure that both rods are installed at exactly the same width and are evenly placed.

2. Measure across one rod from end to end, including the curves. Then add 2 inches to this width measurement to allow for edge finishings. Measure the height from the very top edge of your upper rod down to the bottom edge of your lower rod. Then add 5 inches to this height measurement to allow for edge finishings and rod casings. Cut the fabric to these dimensions.

3. Place the fabric right side down and fold one of the side edges over ½ inch, wrong sides together, and iron in place.

4. Fold over another ½ inch and iron again.

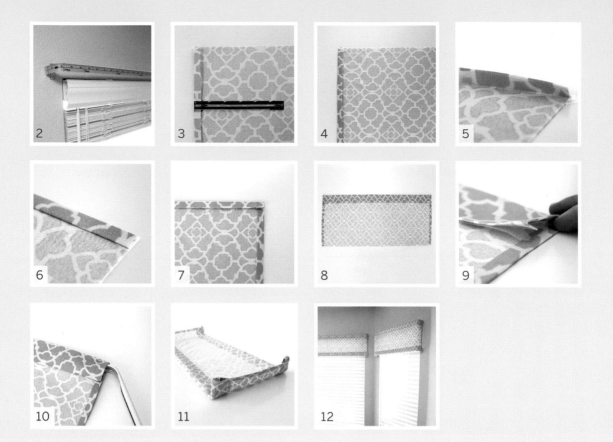

5. Place a strip of fusible adhesive tape beneath the second fold, along the entire length of the side.

6. Iron the fold according to the adhesive's package instructions. Avoid pulling or dragging the iron across the fabric. Repeat steps 3 through 6 on the opposite side of the fabric.

7. Fold the top edge over ½ inch and iron in place.

8. Then fold over 2 inches and iron in place.

9. Place a strip of adhesive under the flap of fabric, lining it up with the bottom folded edge. Iron in place until the fabric is sealed closed. Repeat steps 7 through 9 with the bottom edge of the fabric.

10. Remove your rods from the wall and slide them inside the top and bottom casings.

11. Adjust the rod widths until the ends are even with the ends of the valance.

12. Reattach both rods to the mounts on the wall.

Tips!

The placement of your valance depends on preference. But a good guide is at least an inch (or more) above your window opening and an inch or two from the opening on each side. Of course, this all depends on what surrounds your window and where your windows are placed on your wall. Experiment a bit before placing your curtain rods.

Valance length can also vary from window to window, but a good place to start is one fifth to one sixth of your window height. So if you have a window that is 60 inches tall, a valance length of 10 to 12 inches is ideal.

Measure as you're ironing the edges of your valance to be sure your dimensions are accurate and that it will cover your curved curtain rods.

Chapter 2

KIDS

ALL-IN-ONE PLAY MAT AND TOY BAG

Skip the toy-clean-up battle with your kids by spreading out this play mat and allowing them to scatter their toys on it while playing. When they're through, simply cinch the cord to gather all the pieces into a neat little toy bag. For simple organization and storage, make separate mats/bags for cars, blocks, dolls, etc.

SKILL LEVEL: I » TIME ESTIMATE: 30 MINUTES

Supplies

- 2 yards fleece fabric (at least 60 inches wide)
- 35 inches cotton string, any variety
- 2 (3-yard-long) pieces cording, ¼ inch thick

Toolkit

- Scissors
- Straight pins
- Measuring tape
- Marker or tailor's chalk

The photos for steps 1 through 4 show a mini version of the play mat to help demonstrate the process more clearly.

1. Cut out a 60 x 60-inch square from your fleece fabric.

2. Tie one end of a piece of string to a straight pin and the other end near the tip of a permanent marker or piece of tailor's chalk. The string should measure exactly 29 inches between the two when pulled taut.

3. Mark the exact middle of the square piece of fleece. Stick the pin on that mark and hold it there firmly with one hand while you pull the string and marker straight out with your other hand, making sure there's no slack in the string. Move the marker around the center point, making a curved line on the fabric as you rotate it around the pin.

4. Continue all the way around until you complete the circle, which should be 58 inches in diameter. Cut out the circle.

5. Measure 2 inches in from the outer edge of the circle (it doesn't matter where along the outer curve of the circle you begin).

6. Pinch a bit of that fabric between your thumb and forefinger to make it easier to cut.

7. Cut a ½-inch slit, perpendicular to the outer edge of the circle, making sure that it's about 2 inches from the edge of the circle.

8. Continue cutting ½-inch slits all the way around the circle, spacing each slit about 2 inches apart.

9. Weave one of your pieces of cording in and out of those slits, all the way around half of the circle. The two ends of the cording should come out on the right side of the fleece. (If you're using a solid-colored fleece, you may not have a right and wrong side to your fabric. If this is the case, just have the two ends come out the same side.)

10. Repeat with the other piece of cording, weaving in and out of the slits in the other half of the circle. Tie the two ends of each piece of cording together, making sure that the knots are both on the same side of the fabric.

11. To close the mat and turn it into a bag, pull both knotted ends to cinch the opening closed.

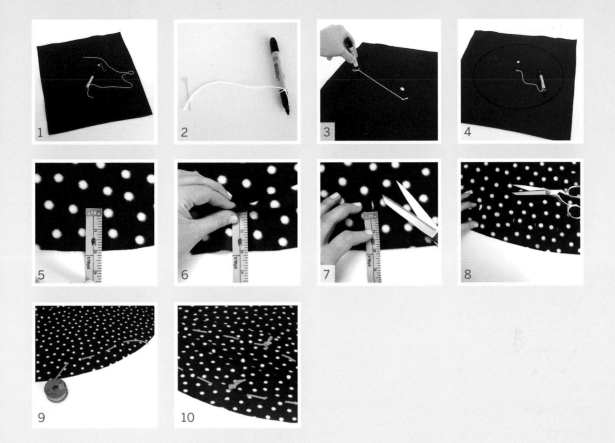

Tips!

If you're using dark fabric, substitute a piece of tailor's chalk for the marker in step 2 so that you can see the line being drawn.

FABRIC MOBILE

Mobiles are good for calming and entertaining babies, and they also make a lovely decorative focal point. And because you're making this yourself, you can create a custom piece of art for any room or lonely corner in your home.

SKILL LEVEL: III   »   TIME ESTIMATE: 3–4 HOURS

Supplies

- 1 (6-inch) and 1 (12-inch) floral craft ring, 1½ inches wide or similar
- Sponge brush or paintbrush
- Acrylic craft paint, any color
- Clear beading wire (non-stretchy)
- 100-percent cotton heavy-duty white quilting thread
- Epoxy glue
- 5 different pieces 100-percent cotton fabric, each ¼ yard long and 44–45 inches wide
- Double-sided fusible adhesive (in sheets or on a roll, with paper on one side)
- 24 (½-inch) crystal beads
- 1 screw hook (for hanging the mobile)

Toolkit

- Power drill
- Scissors
- Ruler
- Iron/ironing board
- Pen or fine-tip marker

*This mobile is meant to be decorative, not interactive. If your child can sit or stand and grab things with his or her hands, be sure that the mobile is out of reach, as the beads can pose a choking hazard.

1. Place your floral craft rings down on the table and be sure the smaller one fits inside the larger one, with room in between.

2. Evenly space and center eight pencil marks around the 6-inch ring and sixteen pencil marks around the 12-inch ring. (You may already have holes in your rings. Use those as a guide and add more if needed.) Use a power drill to make holes through the rings, at each centered pencil mark.

3. Paint each ring with your sponge brush and craft paint. Let dry and then apply a second coat. Let dry.

4. Place the smaller ring inside the larger one and space it evenly. Using either clear beading wire or white quilting thread, tie the two rings together at each quarter section of the rings. Make sure the thread is tight and is keeping the smaller circle securely attached to the larger one. Tie several knots to keep the thread from coming undone.

5. Rotate the thread so that the knots are on the inside of the smaller ring and trim the ends.

6. Place a dab of epoxy glue on each knot to keep the thread in place and to keep the knots from coming undone.

7. Cut your first piece of fabric in half and place one half on an ironing board with the right side facing down. Cut a piece of double-sided adhesive the same size and place the shiny side onto the fabric and the paper side face up. Iron it according to the adhesive's package instructions.

8. Cut out a paper circle (approximately 1¾ inches in diameter) to use as a pattern or find a similarly shaped bowl or lid to trace around. (I used a lid from a spice container.) Trace forty circles onto the paper side of your adhesive.

9. Cut out each circle.

10. When you peel back the paper off each circle, you'll see that the shiny adhesive has adhered to the fabric.

11. Trace forty more circles onto the other half of the fabric, without any adhesive on it.

12. Cut those circles out as well, and make two nice stacks of circles, one with adhesive and one without.

13. Repeat steps 7 through 12 with the other four fabric pieces.

14. Each string of circles hanging from your mobile can vary from seven to ten circles. Decide how many circles you'd like for the first string and place the circles in a line with the adhesive face up and each circle spaced ½ inch apart. Place a matching circle (without adhesive) right next to its fabric mate, with the right side of the fabric facing up. Place a piece of quilting thread across the adhesive circles, with at least a 6-inch tail at each end.

15. Starting at one end of the line of circles, center the thread in the middle of the first adhesive circle, place the matching non-adhesive circle on top, right side up, and fuse them together with a hot iron according to the adhesive's package instructions. Avoid pulling or dragging the iron across the fabric.

16. Continue down the row, fusing all your circles together with the thread sandwiched between the front and back pieces, keeping the circles evenly spaced ½ inch apart. Decide on the number of circles you'd like to add to the other twenty-three rows (between seven and ten circles per row) and where you'd like them to hang and then repeat steps 14 through 16 for each row.

17. Thread one of your strings of circles onto the ring through one of the drilled holes and tie a knot on the under side of the ring. Trim the loose end off and add a dab of glue, just like in step 6. Repeat with the other twenty-three strings of circles.

18. Thread a crystal bead onto the end of one of the string tails and knot it in place about an inch below the lowest fabric circle.

19. Repeat with the other twenty-three strings of circles.

20. Loop a piece of clear beading wire around the larger ring in three different locations. Gather all the clear wire ends, make sure the mobile hangs evenly from them, and then tie the ends into a knot. Loop another long piece of clear wire under the knot you just created and tie the long ends together.

21. Hang from a screw hook.

1

2

3

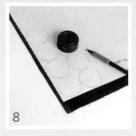

4

5

6

7

8

9

10

11

12

13

14

15

16

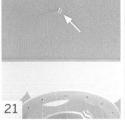

Tips!

If you are unable to locate floral craft rings, consider using embroidery hoops or something similar.

To make the holes in the rings with a power drill, place a ring on top of two stacks of books and drill through the space between the books.

You can use more or fewer fabric colors, but you'll need to adjust the number of circles you cut out.

Keep in mind that you have twenty-four total holes, between the small and large rings, to hang fabric circles from. Before fusing your circles together, consider laying out each of the twenty-four lines of circles on the table and varying the color choices and number of circles for each line. That way, you can get a visual representation of your color choices and lengths for each line of your mobile before you tie them on.

Don't drag the iron across the fabric; lift and press to avoid fabric shifting.

If some of the circles happen to come loose from the string while you're working and putting things together, slide them back into place and iron again.

SIPPY CUP LEASH

Have you ever been on a walk, in the car, or eating a meal and your little one thinks it's a funny game to keep throwing her sippy cup onto the ground? Yeah, not so funny. Create a little leash for the sippy cup, and you'll eliminate the pick-up-the-sippy-100-times game. When your little one throws it, the cup will just hang from the end of the ribbon, ready for the next time she's thirsty. Genius.

SKILL LEVEL: 1 » TIME ESTIMATE: 20 MINUTES

Supplies

- 10 to 15 inches elastic, 1 inch wide
- Sippy cup (narrow at the middle, wider at top and bottom)
- Epoxy glue
- 38 inches grosgrain ribbon, 1 inch wide

Toolkit

- Scissors
- Measuring tape
- Clothespins or a heavy book
- Lighter

1. Wrap elastic around the middle of the sippy cup to measure how much you'll need. Hold the elastic nice and firm around the middle of the cup. While still holding the elastic firmly, slide the elastic off the cup and back on again, to be sure the elastic is not too tight but is still a snug fit. Allow for 1½ inches extra at each end of the elastic and cut off any excess beyond that.

2. Place a line of epoxy glue on each end of the elastic, measuring 1½ inches from the cut ends. Fold the elastic in half so that the glued ends meet.

3. Press the ends together firmly until dried completely. (Placing a book on top or securing with clothespins is helpful for adding pressure while drying.)

4. Using a lighter, carefully singe the cut ends of the ribbon to keep them from fraying. The ribbon should melt instantly, sealing the fraying ends.

5. Fold the ribbon in half, matching up the two cut ends. Slide the glued ends of the elastic between the two ends of ribbon, with the ribbon covering the double layer of elastic by 1½ inches. Place glue on both sides of the elastic and sandwich the ribbon around it on both sides. Adjust the sides of the ribbon and elastic quickly, as needed, making sure they all line up. Apply pressure and let dry.

6. Glue the loop of ribbon closed, making a double-layered "leash," stopping 4 inches from the looped end. Match up the edges of the ribbon as needed, press firmly closed, and let dry completely before using.

7. Place the ribbon end under a strap or bar on the stroller and pass the elastic end through the loop and pull until secure. Slide the cup into the elastic end and make sure you have a snug fit.

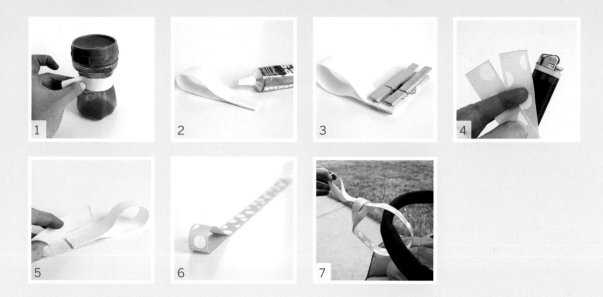

Tips!

If your child puts things in her mouth pretty often and you're concerned about her possibly ingesting part of the dried epoxy glue, use double-sided fusible adhesive tape in place of the glue and construct the leash in the same way.

FLIP-FLOP HEEL STRAPS

If you're thiiiiis close to throwing away your child's flip-flops because he can't keep them on his feet (and his feet no longer fit in the flip-flop sizes with the back strap), take a deep breath and keep them out of the trash can. You can create your own stretchy heel straps! And then your little one can dance, skip, and hop without his flip-flops flying off his feet.

SKILL LEVEL: I » **TIME ESTIMATE: 30 MINUTES**

Supplies

- 24–30 inches fold-over elastic, ⅝ inch wide (decorative elastic, if available)
- 4 (⅜ inch) metal snap sets
- Snap hammer tool (or other snap tool)
- Pair of flip-flops

Toolkit

- Scissors
- Measuring tape
- Pen or fine-tip marker
- Hammer
- Lighter

*Keep in mind that the length of elastic you need depends on the size of foot you're making the straps for and the type of elastic you use. (All elastics stretch a little differently.)

1. In order to complete two heel straps, you'll need sixteen snap pieces total: four sockets (*a*), four studs (*b*), and eight open ring prongs (*c*). You'll also need a hammer tool (*d*).

2. Cut a piece of elastic that's 12 inches long and carefully heat-seal one cut end with a lighter. (This will melt the end and keep it from unraveling.)

3. Fold the melted end of your elastic over ¾ inch.

4. Place the spikes of one ring prong through the front of the elastic, poking through the two layers of folded elastic and coming out the back side. (The ring prong sitting to the right in the photo is there to show you which piece is being used in this step.)

5. Place a stud piece right on top of the prongs.

6. Place and center the hammer tool on top of the stud piece. Tap a regular hammer on top of the hammer tool, compressing the two metal pieces together.

7. Place the corresponding socket piece about 1 inch away from the stud piece, by first pushing the ring prong through from the right side and then setting the socket piece on the ring prong and using the hammer tool to compress them together.

8. Loop this end around the side of the flip-flop strap and snap in place. Have your child put the flip-flop on and then pull the other end of the elastic around his heel and slip it through the other side of the flip-flop strap. Pull the elastic so that it's snug and will keep the flip-flop in place and then mark where the elastic folds around the flip-flop strap. Let the elastic relax and then measure 2 inches out from where you marked the elastic. Cut off the excess elastic.

9. Unsnap the elastic from the flip-flop and attach another snap set to the other end of the elastic, the same way you did with the first (which makes the heel straps adjustable).

10. Loop both ends around each side of the flip-flop and snap in place.

Tips!

Fold-over elastic is soft and won't irritate skin, and that's why it's used for this project. If you can't find any, look for another type of elastic that's on the softer side.

Fold-over elastic can be purchased in lots of fun prints and designs; however, it is sometimes hard to find in local stores. You may need to look for "elastic trim" in order to find it. (Or order it online.)

If you can't find ⅝-inch-wide elastic, anything between ⅜ inch and about 1 inch will work.

The spacing of your snaps that fit around the flip-flop strap will vary, depending on the width of the flip-flop strap. Adjust accordingly.

SUN HAT CHIN STRAP

Baby sun hats generally come with a chin strap to keep the baby from yanking the hat off. But how about toddlers or babies with larger heads? The larger sizes just aren't made very often with chin straps. Don't get frustrated with the lack of options available at the store— just make your own!

SKILL LEVEL: II » **TIME ESTIMATE: 30 MINUTES**

Supplies

- Grosgrain ribbon, ⅝ inch wide (amount depends on head size)
- Double-sided fusible adhesive tape, ½ inch wide
- 5 (⅜-inch) metal snap sets
- Snap hammer tool (or other snap tool)
- Sun hat

Toolkit

- Scissors
- Measuring tape
- Iron/ironing board
- Lighter
- Hammer

Every child's head size is a little different, so measurements will vary. Cut your ribbon longer than you think you'll need and then, after trying it on and before adding snaps, trim off the excess.

1. The straps that come under the chin will fasten off to one side. The longer section that goes under the chin is about twice the length of the shorter side. Remember to cut the ribbon longer than you think you will need. You can always trim it down. If you're unsure where to even start, for toddler size, cut two ribbons 7 inches long each and two ribbons 14 inches long each. If they're too long (which they most likely will be), you can trim later.

2. Lay the two shorter ribbons down in front of you and place a strip of fusible adhesive tape along the entire length of one of the ribbons. (If your ribbon has a print on it, place the adhesive on the wrong side of the ribbon.)

3. Place the other ribbon on top (right side up, if applicable), keeping the sides and ends even. Iron the layers together according to the adhesive's package instructions. Repeat with the two longer ribbons.

4. Carefully heat-seal all the cut ends of the ribbon with a lighter to keep them from fraying.

5. Gather your snap pieces and tools for attaching the straps. You'll need a hammer tool (or other snap tool, *a*) and twelve total snap pieces: five sockets, (*b*), one stud, (*c*), and six open ring prongs, (*d*).

6. Measure to find the two center points on the sides of the hat and place a short piece of ribbon on the inside of the hat, at one of those points. Hold the ribbon there with your finger, just to see exactly where you'd like it to be attached.

7. Place one of your open ring prongs on the outside of the hat, where you're holding the ribbon strap on the inside, with the prongs facing down.

8. Let go of the ribbon for now and push the prongs through the fabric of the hat (this will take some wiggling and maneuvering), until they poke through on the inside of the hat.

9. Take the shorter ribbon strap and fold over one end ⅝ inch. (Folding the end under will give it a polished look and will also keep the possibly irritating melted end away from the face.)

10. Place the folded end of the ribbon onto the prongs that are poking through the hat, making sure that the folded end of the ribbon is facing down (and is hidden). Center it over the prongs and press the ribbon down onto the prongs the best you can.

11. Place a socket piece on top of the ribbon and prongs and set the hammer tool on top of the socket piece. Tap a regular hammer on top of the hammer tool, compressing the two metal pieces together.

Place the longer ribbon on the opposite side of the hat on the inside, attaching it to the hat with your snap pieces just like you did with the shorter ribbon.

12. Place the hat on your child and see if the ribbons are at a good length, keeping in mind you'll be folding the ends under ⅝ inch. Trim if necessary. Fold the end of your short ribbon under ⅝ inch, toward the inside of the hat.

13. Attach the stud piece to this end of the ribbon, making sure that you press the prong piece through the side that's folded over so that the socket piece will end up on the outside of the ribbon (and facing the outside of the hat) when the hat is being worn.

14. Fold the end of the long ribbon under ⅝ inch, toward the inside of the hat. Then add a socket piece to the end, with the socket facing toward the inside of the hat. Add two more socket pieces to the ribbon, spacing them about a ¼ inch apart, to allow for adjustments as your child grows.

Tips!

Five metal snap sets are required for this project, but not all parts will be used. Snaps generally come in sets, and you need at least five of one part of the set, which is why five sets are called for. Save the extra pieces for another project.

If you are having a hard time getting the snaps through your hat and ribbon, consider leaving the ribbon end unfolded (and trim off the excess), eliminating some bulk.

2

3

4

d

a

b

c

5

6

7

8

9

10

11

12

13

14

PACIFIER CLIP

If you know babies, you know that pacifiers fall out of their mouths approximately, oh, forty-seven times a day. To keep the pacifier from falling to the ground or to avoid losing it completely, secure it to a clip and attach the clip to the baby's clothing. Crisis averted!

SKILL LEVEL: I   »   TIME ESTIMATE: 20 MINUTES

Supplies

- 8 inches grosgrain ribbon, ½–⅞ inch wide
- 2 (⅜-inch) metal snap sets
- Snap hammer tool (or other snap tool)
- 1 suspender clip with a 1-inch-wide opening
- Pacifier

Toolkit

- Scissors
- Measuring tape
- Lighter
- Hammer
- Pen or fine-tip marker

1. In order to make one pacifier clip, you'll need eight snap pieces and a hammer tool (or other snap tool, a): two sockets (b), two studs (c), and four open ring prongs (d).

2. Carefully heat-seal the two ends of your piece of ribbon with a lighter. (This will keep the ribbon from fraying.)

3. Place the spikes of one ring prong through the right side (if you have one) of the ribbon end, poking out through the back of the ribbon, about ⅛ inch from the end of the ribbon.

4. Place the socket piece on top of the prongs.

5. Place and center the hammer tool on top of the socket piece.

6. Tap a regular hammer on top of the hammer tool, compressing the two metal pieces together.

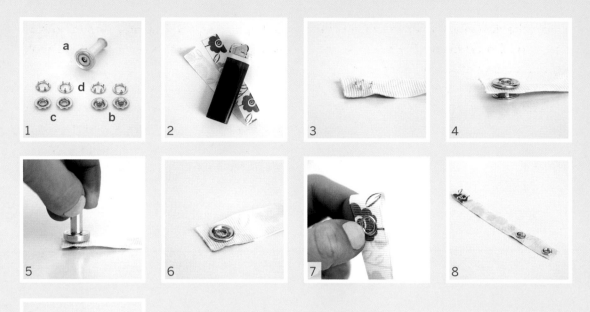

7. Fold the ribbon end over 1 inch and mark where you'll need to attach the corresponding stud piece so that both snap pieces line up together. Attach the stud piece in the same way you attached the socket.

8. Repeat steps 3 through 7 with the other end of the ribbon to attach the other set of snap pieces.

9. Slide the suspender clip through one end of the ribbon and fasten the snap closed. Loop the other end through your pacifier and snap closed.

Tips!

If your pacifier doesn't have a handle or slot to thread the ribbon through, some pacifier brands offer an adapter piece for this exact purpose. If not, try using a different type of pacifier.

COLORED PENCIL ROLL-UP

When colored pencils (or any other writing utensils) have a designated "home," they are less likely to end up on the floor or in the junk drawer. Make a few slits into a piece of vinyl, slide your pencils inside their individual slots, roll the whole thing up, tie it closed . . . and thank me later for a little less clutter in your life!

SKILL LEVEL: I   »   TIME ESTIMATE: 60–90 MINUTES

Supplies

- ¼ yard vinyl (faux leather)
- White colored pencil or narrow tailor's chalk
- 1 yard grosgrain ribbon, 1½ inches wide
- Epoxy glue

Toolkit

- Scissors
- Measuring tape
- Utility knife
- Cutting mat
- Lighter

This colored pencil roll-up is designed to fit standard 7-inch-long colored pencils that are ¼ inch in diameter. If you'd rather create a roll-up for crayons or pens, make adjustments accordingly.

1. Cut your piece of vinyl down to 8¼ x 23 inches.

2. Use a white colored pencil or narrow tailor's chalk to draw two lines down the length of the fabric on the wrong side, splitting the 8¼-inch width of the fabric into exact thirds. (Each third will be 2¾ inches wide.)

3. Turn the fabric so that the white lines are horizontal and place the fabric on top of a cutting mat. Measure in from the left side 1½ inches along the bottom white line and then make a ¾-inch slit with a utility knife, right along the white line. Make another identical ¾-inch slit, ¼ inch below the first one.

4. Continue making pairs of ¾-inch slits along the bottom white line that are spaced ¼ inch apart. You will make a total of twenty pairs of slits along the white line, stopping 1½ inches from the other end.

5. These sets of slits will create a snug home for one end of your colored pencils to rest.

6. Repeat the same process with the upper white line, creating ¾-inch slits right along the line, but with the corresponding identical slit ¼ inch above the white line rather than below.

7. The slits along both the upper and lower white lines should match up evenly so that there is a place for each end of your colored pencil.

8. Take your 1-yard piece of ribbon and carefully heat-seal both ends with a lighter to melt them and keep them from fraying.

9. Find the middle of the piece of ribbon and then apply a generous amount of epoxy glue to the wrong side (if applicable) in a 1½ x 1½-inch square.

10. Lay the vinyl down in front of you horizontally, with the right side facing up. Place the glue-covered section of the ribbon facedown, at one end of the vinyl, centering it from top to bottom (use the arrows on photo 10 as a guide for placement). Press firmly and let dry completely before using.

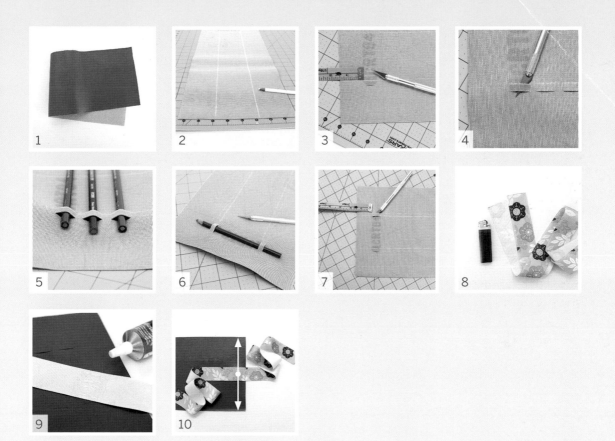

Tips!

If you have some real leather and prefer to use it for this project, go right ahead! Faux leather is just less expensive, is easier to find in bigger pieces, and comes in a variety of colors.

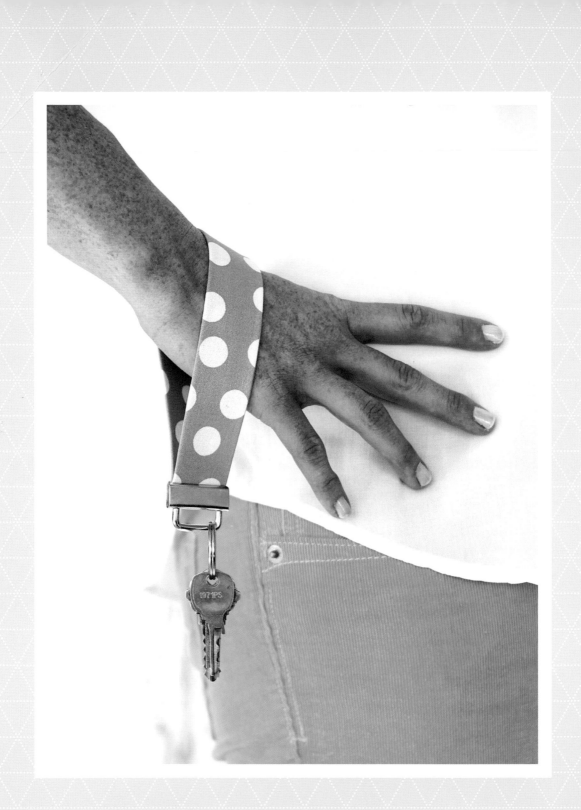

Chapter 3

ACCESSORIES

WOVEN CLUTCH

For the times when all you have are a few items to carry with you, skip the big bulky purse and carry around this darling clutch instead. It has a simple Velcro closure and fits nicely in your hand, keeping your keys, phone, and money at your fingertips. No one will believe you made it yourself, and without a single strand of thread!

SKILL LEVEL: III » TIME ESTIMATE: 90 MINUTES

Supplies

- 11 yards jute ribbon, ⅝ inch wide
- ¼ yard cotton fabric
- Hot glue gun and glue sticks
- 1½ yards grosgrain ribbon, ⅜ inch wide
- Double-sided fusible adhesive (in sheets or on a roll, with paper on one side)
- 4 inches Velcro, ½–1 inch wide
- Epoxy glue

Toolkit

- Scissors
- Masking tape
- Measuring tape
- Iron/ironing board

The finished clutch measures approximately 8 x 5 inches.

1. Cut eleven strips of your jute ribbon, each 15 inches long. Line them up in a row vertically, as close as possible without overlapping, and place a piece of masking tape along the top ½ inch of the ribbons to hold them in place on your work surface.

2. Weave a piece of jute ribbon horizontally through the eleven strips, first going over and then going under. Repeat until the entire row has been woven.

3. Let the ends of this horizontal piece extend ½ inch on each edge. Cut off the excess ribbon. Place a piece of tape at each end to hold the ribbon in place.

4. Begin weaving your next row of ribbon, first going under and then going over. Let the ends extend ½ inch on each end. Cut off the excess ribbon. Place tape to hold the ½-inch ends in place.

5. As you weave each row of ribbon, alternating between starting with going over or under, you'll need to adjust the rows with your fingers so that they fit together tightly.

After you've woven sixteen rows of ribbon, stop.

6. Cut a piece of cotton fabric that measures 2½ x 9 inches. Fold it in half lengthwise, with wrong sides together, and iron flat.

7. Open it up, fold both long edges in to meet the center fold, and iron both sides flat. Fold back in half along the original long fold, and iron the whole strip flat again. (The folded fabric should measure about ⅝ inch wide and be four layers thick.)

8. Use this strip of fabric to weave your next row. Tape both ½-inch ends down, just like you did with the jute ribbon.

9. Add one more row of jute ribbon below the row of fabric, checking to be sure the height of your weaving section is about 13 inches. (It may be a little more or less,

depending on how tightly or loosely you wove your ribbon.)

10. Place a long strip of tape along the bottom edges of the vertical pieces, securing them in place.

11. Peel up the edges of the tape, trying to keep the ribbons connected as one piece, and then flip the whole woven piece over. Begin hot gluing your grosgrain ribbon along one edge of the woven rectangle, right along the inside edges of the tape lines.

12. Continue along all four sides of the rectangle shape.

13. Flip it back over and trim off the excess edges of jute ribbon and tape, right up to the ribbon you just glued in place.

14. Cut a piece of cotton fabric exactly the same size as the woven piece.

15. Use the fabric piece as a template for cutting a piece of fusible adhesive the same size.

16. Place the fabric piece in front of you with the wrong side facing up and then place the adhesive with the shiny side facing down on top of the fabric (the paper side should be facing up). Match up the sides and edges of these two pieces and then fuse them together with an iron according to the adhesive's package instructions. Avoid pulling or dragging the iron across the fabric.

17. Peel the paper backing of the adhesive off the fabric. (If the paper backing is not separating from the adhesive, you need to repeat the last step and iron it a little longer.)

18. Place the adhesive side of the fabric onto the back side of the woven rectangle, covering the ribbon-bound edges.

19. Fuse the layers together with an iron.

20. You should now have one layer of material with woven ribbon on the front and fabric on the back.

21. Cut a piece of jute ribbon that's slightly longer than the bottom edge (the shorter side without the woven fabric strip) of your rectangle. Hot glue the ribbon down along the bottom edge of the woven rectangle, gluing half of the ribbon's width and leaving the other half as overhang.

22. Fold the other half of the ribbon width to the back side of the woven rectangle, hot gluing this edge down along the fabric. Trim off the excess ribbon from both ends, if applicable.

23. With the rectangle piece still ribbon side facedown in front of you, fold the bottom edge up 4½ inches. Press flat with your fingers, creating a fold along the bottom as best you can. Place a thin line of hot glue along both inside edges, in between the two layers that you just folded. (Use the arrows on photo 23 as a guide for placement.) This will create a pocket in your clutch.

24. Cut a piece of jute ribbon 10 inches long and fold over one end about ½ inch and glue in place.

25. Place the folded end facedown onto one long side of your woven piece, lining up the folded end with the bottom edge. Hot glue half of the ribbon width along the woven piece. Trim off the excess length from the other end of ribbon.

26. Fold the other half of the ribbon width to the back side of the woven piece, hot gluing this edge down along the fabric. Be sure that the ribbon is evenly wrapped around the front and back. Repeat steps 24 through 26 with the other long side of the rectangle piece.

27. Sandwich one last piece of jute ribbon around the final edge of your rectangle piece, making sure both ends of the ribbon are folded under ½ inch to hide the cut ends (refer to step 24).

28. Fold the top edge down like a business letter. Iron the crease gently, avoiding the areas with glue.

29. Cut two 2-inch pieces of Velcro and attach them to the underside of the top flap of the clutch with epoxy glue. Attach their corresponding Velcro pieces to the pouch, right where they would meet with the flap closed.

30. Cut a piece of cotton fabric that measures 7 x 4 inches. Fold the two long sides toward the center, with wrong sides together, overlapping them by about 1 inch (making it about 1½ inches wide). Press flat with your fingers.

31. Fold both ends in toward the center again, overlapping by ½ inch (making it about 3¼ inches wide). Press flat with your fingers. (Add a dot of glue to hold the flaps in place, if needed.)

32. With the overlapped edges toward the back, pinch the middle with your fingers, creating a bow shape. Set aside.

33. Cut another piece of cotton fabric to 1¾ x 4 inches. Fold the two long 4-inch sides toward the center, overlapping them by about ¼ inch (making it about ¾ inch wide). Iron flat.

34. Pinch the middle of the bow like you did previously. Glue one end of the smaller piece (with the folds facing down) to the back side of the bow.

Add a little more glue to the back side of the strip as you wrap it around the front of the bow.

35. Cut off the excess fabric from the strip and glue the end to the back of the bow.

36. Attach your bow to the front of the clutch with a generous amount of hot glue, without letting it ooze into sight.

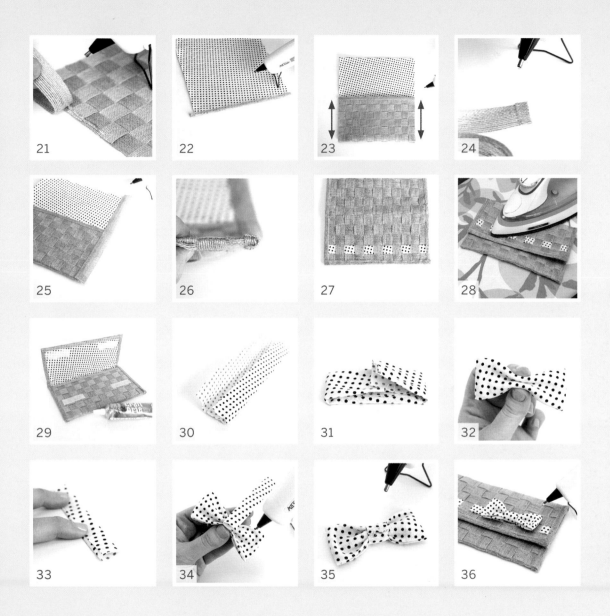

Tips!

If you can't find jute ribbon, you can make this clutch with any other sturdy type of ribbon, such as grosgrain.

Be careful when ironing any parts of this clutch that have been hot glued. The glue will melt again under a hot iron, and that equals a sticky mess!

BRAIDED LEATHER HEADBAND

Do you tire of hair flyaways? Fix that problem lickety-split with some braided leather. Even if you don't suffer from flyaways, these braided headbands are the perfect hair accessory.

SKILL LEVEL: I » TIME ESTIMATE: 30 MINUTES

Supplies

- 90 inches leather cord, ⅛ inch thick
- Cotton string
- 3½ inches fold-over elastic
- 2 (2½-inch) pieces grosgrain ribbon, 1 inch wide
- Hot glue gun and glue sticks

Toolkit

- Scissors
- Flexible measuring tape
- Lighter
- Masking tape

1. Cut three pieces of leather cord, each 30 inches long.

2. Tie the leather cords tightly together at one end with cotton string. Leave about an inch of loose cord ends above the string knot.

3. Tape the short loose cord ends down to the table in front of you with some masking tape. Begin braiding, trying to keep the leather pieces as flat and uniform as you can.

4. Continue braiding until you reach the length of braid that you need for your head and then tie the ends tightly together with more string. To determine a proper fit, measure around the head where a headband sits, all the way around the head. Subtract 4 inches from that measurement for the total length of your leather braid. After tying off the end of the braid, cut the excess cord, leaving only ½ inch of excess cord below the tied string. Take the tape off the top excess cords and cut those down to ½ inch too.

5. Use a lighter to carefully heat-seal the ends of your fold-over elastic. This will melt the ends and keep them from unraveling.

6. Place your elastic vertically on the table in front of you. Place your braid down above the elastic and overlap the bottom end of the braid onto the elastic, by ⅞ inch. Place a 2½-inch piece of ribbon perpendicular to the overlapped cord and elastic, making sure that the overlap isn't longer than the width of the ribbon. You'll be wrapping the ribbon around this section, and you want all to be hidden. Tie more cotton string around the elastic and cording, securing them together nice and tight. Trim off the excess cotton string. This will be the back side of the headband.

7. Add a generous dot of hot glue between the ends of the cording and elastic.

8. Pinch the elastic around the cord ends and let the glue dry completely.

9. Apply a line of glue to one end of your ribbon piece . . .

10. . . . and place the glue side down onto where the cording and elastic meet. Be sure that the ribbon is covering all cord and elastic ends.

11. Wrap the ribbon around the cording and elastic as tightly as you can. Wrap until the ribbon overlaps itself by about ¼ inch. Cut off excess ribbon.

12. Use a lighter to carefully heat-seal the end of the ribbon.

13. Glue the end in place with hot glue. Repeat steps 6 through 13 to attach the elastic and braid on the other side, making sure they aren't twisted before securing the ends together.

Tips!

Sometimes it's difficult to find leather cording in a variety of colors in local stores. Try looking online—the selection is huge!

All elastics behave a little differently. Some stretch more and some less. For this reason, you may need to adjust the length of elastic used.

If you prefer not to use hot glue, epoxy glue would work great for this as well. It just takes longer to dry and requires more pinching and holding while the glue dries.

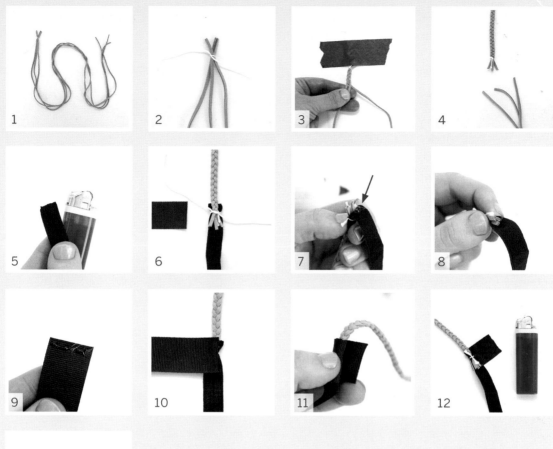

FABRIC FLOWER

Adding a flower can turn a "cute" project into an "oh-my-word-that's-ADORABLE" project. And this flower can be made from new fabric or from cut scraps of old T-shirts or past projects.

SKILL LEVEL: I » TIME ESTIMATE: 30 MINUTES

Supplies

- ⅛ yard cotton knit fabric (or an old T-shirt)
- White felt
- Hot glue gun and glue sticks
- Jewel, button, or other notion for flower center

Optional Supplies

- 1-inch cover button kit
- Headband

Toolkit

- Scissors
- Ruler

1. Cut out eight circles from your knit fabric: four that are 2¾ inches in diameter and four that are 2¼ inches in diameter. Then cut a 1½-inch-diameter circle from the felt.

2. Place a small dot of hot glue in the center of one of the knit circles (either size).

3. Fold in half and press down in the center where the glue dot is, to keep the circle folded in half.

4. Place a dot of glue at the center of the folded side of your circle.

5. Fold in half again, pressing down on the glue dot to keep the fabric folded in place.

6. Repeat with the other seven knit circles.

7. Arrange the four larger quartered circles evenly on the felt circle and glue them down.

1

2

3

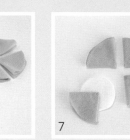

4

5

6

7

8

9

10

1

2

3

4

8. Arrange the smaller quartered circle pieces on top, slightly shifting the placement of each section to sit directly above two of the larger sections below. Glue them in place.

9. With each quartered piece you glue down, be sure to add enough glue so that it will stay in place, but not so much that it oozes out or becomes too bulky.

10. Arrange the center embellishment on the flower and glue it down.

Additional Instructions

1. For extra dimension (and before adding the embellishment to the center of the flower), you can add another layer of four circles that are cut to 1¾ inches diameter.

2. If you'd like to add a cover button to the center of the flower, follow the package instructions on your particular kit.

3. If your cover button includes a shank on the back, bend that over the best you can so that it will lie flat on the flower.

4. If you'd like to attach the flower to a headband, hot glue the back side of the flower to any headband style. Then glue a small felt circle to the back of the flower, sandwiching the headband in between the two felt circles. (If your headband is extra wide and hides the back of the flower completely, you can skip the extra felt circle.)

Tips!

Knit fabric is used for these flowers because knit fabric is cool like that and it won't fray! However, you can also make these from regular woven cotton, and they should only fray minimally because they are cut into circles. (Circular cuts are like bias cuts and keep fraying to a minimum.) If you like a shabbier flower, using a woven cotton is ideal!

When you cut your circles, they don't have to be exact or perfectly round. In fact, uneven edges give the flower petals a little more dimension and shape.

LEATHER FRINGE NECKLACE

It's crazy how something as simple as a little leather detail can do so much for your ward-robe. This Leather Fringe Necklace can be made in minutes and will instantly dress an outfit up or down. Go on, give it a try!

SKILL LEVEL: I » TIME ESTIMATE: 15 MINUTES

Supplies

- Leather scrap (at least 1½ x 5 inches)
- Necklace chain (color and length depend on personal preference)
- Epoxy glue

Toolkit

- Scissors
- Ruler
- Clothespins or a heavy book

1. Cut a piece of leather that is 1½ x 5 inches.

2. Cut off the corners at each end of your rectangle.

3. Place the leather right side down in front of you and drape your necklace chain across the middle of the leather piece. Fold the leather in half (just about), letting the back half hang down a little longer than the front. Open it back up and add a narrow line of epoxy glue across the leather, right below the necklace chain. (Just don't add too much glue, or it will ooze onto the necklace chain.)

4. Fold the top half of the leather back down and apply pressure to the glue (with clothespins or a heavy book) until it dries.

5. Cut slits in the leather along the front layer, making sure that you don't cut through the line of glue that's underneath.

6. Repeat with the back layer of leather, cutting the slits the same width as the front layer.

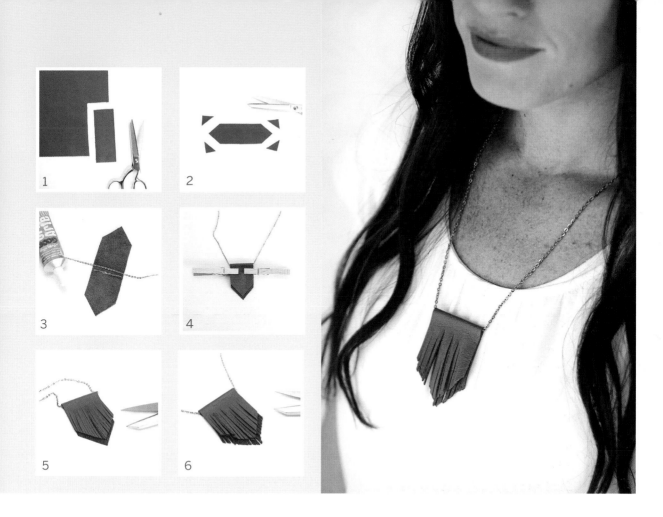

Tips!

Stretching and pulling on your leather fringes will help give the leather some shape and dimension. But don't use your superhero muscles, or you'll rip the fringes right off!

If you can't find any leather to purchase by the yard, check out the thrift store (or your closet) for old leather purses or jackets. You only need a little bit, so it can be cut from anything.

HAIR BOW CLIP WITH NO-SLIP GRIP

No more cursing at those darn baby hair bows for falling out of your baby's silky fine hair. Make your own bows with a bit of non-slip grip, and let others make no mistake that your baby is indeed a girl. They're great for bigger girls too!

SKILL LEVEL: II » TIME ESTIMATE: 30 MINUTES

Supplies

- 1 (5-inch) piece of ribbon, ⅜ inch wide
- Hot glue gun and glue sticks
- 1 double-prong hair clip, 1¾ inches long
- 3 (4-inch) pieces of ribbon, ⅜ inch wide
- 1 (1¼ x ⅓-inch) piece of shelf liner
- 1 (1¼ x ⅓-inch) piece of white felt

Toolkit

- Scissors
- Ruler
- Lighter

1. Gather your supplies for making one simple hair bow.

2. Grab your 5-inch piece of ribbon and carefully heat-seal one end of it with a lighter by holding the flame on the raw edge for a brief moment. This will melt the end just a bit and keep it from fraying.

3. Add a bit of hot glue to the wrong side of the ribbon end you just heat-sealed and place it on the bottom edge of the clip, overlapping by about ⅜ inch. Press firmly.

4. Add another line of glue (an inch or so) to the next section of the wrong side of the ribbon.

5. Press firmly against the contour of the pinch end of the clip.

6. Measure how much more ribbon you'll need to finish off the clip by stretching the ribbon to the tip of the clip prongs and then folding it back up the length of the prongs. Cut off the excess.

7. Heat-seal the other end of the ribbon.

8. Add another line of hot glue down the wrong side of the rest of the ribbon.

9. Finish putting the ribbon in place on top of the prongs and back underneath. Press firmly in place.

10. Grab your three 4-inch pieces of ribbon. Tie a single knot in the center of one of the pieces of ribbon. Try to make it a neat little knot and keep the two ends flat and laying in the same direction as you pull. Set aside. Carefully heat-seal the ends of the two un-knotted pieces of ribbon.

11. Loop each of the two un-knotted pieces of ribbon into a circle, overlap the ends by ⅜ inch, and glue them together with more hot glue.

12. Pinch one of the circles right in the center and add a little dot of hot glue to the inside center to keep it pinched together. Repeat with the other circle of ribbon.

13. Cross the two pieces together—not into an actual "X" but more like a squashed one. Add a dot of hot glue between the two to keep them together.

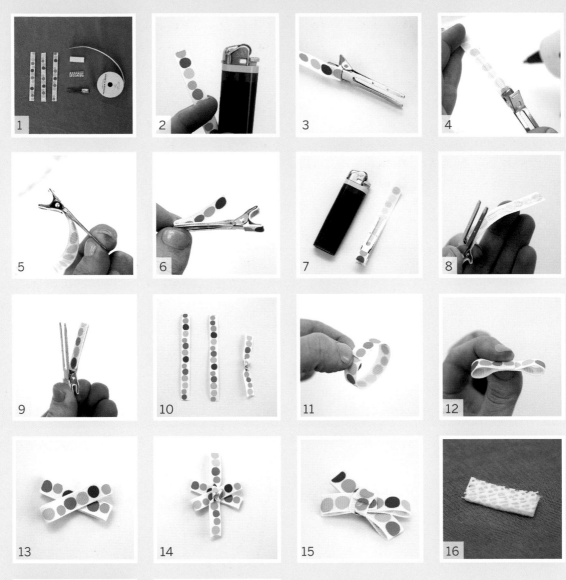

14. Place the piece of ribbon with the knot in the middle in the center of the squashed "X," with the right side of the ribbon facing up. Place a dot of hot glue under the knot so it doesn't move around.

15. Turn the bow over and cut off the long ends of the knotted ribbon just a bit and glue them down to the back side of the bow.

16. To make your hair clip "no-slip," glue the shelf liner piece to the felt piece and squeeze them together so they become one piece. (Caution: This can burn your fingers. Wait until the glue has cooled from hot to warm and then test carefully with your fingers.) Cut off uneven edges.

17. Place some glue on the felt side, attach it to the top prongs of the clip, and press firmly in place.

18. Glue the back side of the bow to the top of the clip, centering the bow in place.

Tips!

Grosgrain ribbon works best for this project; however, other types of ribbon can be used with a little more patience.

Shelf liner comes in different thicknesses. Choose one that isn't so thick it fills the prongs but is thick enough to make the clip grip the hair.

These basic bows can be added to any sort of clip or barrette, but my preference (for little girls with very little or fine hair) is to use a double-prong metal hair clip.

BASIC TOTE

Who doesn't need another tote? I have a whole stash of them, but when I find a new fabric print that I just have to have, I always find myself making another tote to carry with me to the lake, to the library, or on a last-minute weekend trip. But giving a tote as a gift, with other goodies stuffed inside, is one of my favorite reasons to make a new one!

SKILL LEVEL: II » TIME ESTIMATE: 90 MINUTES

Supplies

- ¾ yard medium-weight cotton (this will be your outer fabric)
- 1 yard medium-weight cotton lining fabric
- Double-sided fusible adhesive tape, ¼ inch wide and ½ inch wide
- Epoxy glue
- 4 (½-inch) metal eyelet sets
- Eyelet setter hammer tool (or other eyelet tool)
- Fabric Flower, page 107 (optional)

Toolkit

- Scissors
- Measuring tape
- Ruler or hem guide ruler
- Iron/ironing board
- Hammer
- Straight pins
- Pen or fine-tip marker

The finished tote measures approximately 15 x 17 inches.

1. Cut two pieces of your outer fabric and two pieces of your lining fabric that are 19½ inches high x 18 inches wide. Cut two handle pieces out of your lining fabric that are 4 x 30 inches each.

2. Place one of your outer fabric pieces in front of you, right side up, with the longer sides on the left and right. Place a piece of ½-inch-wide fusible adhesive tape along both sides and the bottom, lining it up exactly with the outer edge. (Use the arrows on photo 2 as a guide for placement.)

3. Place the other outer fabric piece on top, right side down. Match up all sides, making sure that the fusible adhesive tape is sandwiched between the two layers as close as possible to the cut edges. Iron in place according to the adhesive's package instructions. Avoid pulling or dragging the iron across the fabric. Now you have three sides fused together, while the top is still open.

4. To make the boxed-out corners for the tote, keep the bag inside out and grab one of the bottom corners. Pull the right sides of the fabric away from each other just a bit, creating a pocket inside of that bottom corner.

5. Line up the side fused seam with the adjacent bottom fused seam by folding it over and press the fabric together and flat. Manipulate it and feel the best you can with your fingers, keeping the bottom and side fused seams exactly in line with each other.

6. Make the corner nice and pointy and place a pin to hold the bottom and side fused seams together. The more even you can keep these two fused seams together, the better your boxed-out corner will look. (In the photo, you are seeing half of the front of the bag and half of the back.)

7. Do the same with the other corner and add a pin as well, to keep the fabric in place.

8. Iron it flat to help keep it in place for the next step.

9. Measure in 2 inches from the pointy corner (not including the excess fabric) and draw a line perpendicular with the line of excess fabric that is running horizontally in the photo.

10. Cut the fabric off, right along the line.

11. Keep the fabric folded the same way, as best as you can, while lifting up the cut opening just a bit. Slide a piece of ½-inch-wide fusible adhesive tape between those two layers of fabric, lining it up with the cut edge. Press it closed again and iron in place. Repeat steps 4 through 11 with the other corner.

12. Turn the bag right side out, revealing your new boxed-out corners.

13. Fold each corner flat, right along the seam where you fused the corner together and press it flat. (This will help it keep its shape a little better.)

14. You may notice that each end has a little gap where the adhesive didn't reach. This is because the fabric was cut at an angle.

15. Add a little epoxy glue to those gaps and pinch shut until completely dry. Repeat with the other corner.

16. Iron the bag along each of the side seams and the bottom seam.

17. Repeat steps 2 through 16 with the lining pieces.

18. Fold the upper edge of the outer fabric down 2 inches (toward the inside of the bag). Pin in place.

19. Do the same with the lining fabric, but then turn it inside out. Press each of the upper edges flat with your iron.

20. Slide the lining fabric inside the outer fabric.

21. Line up the upper edges and pin, making sure that the two side seams are matched up at each side.

22. Carefully unpin one side of the upper edge of the tote and place two strips of ½-inch-wide fusible adhesive tape between the two layers. Place one line of tape along the very top folded edge and the other about an inch below that, for extra strength. Pin the two layers back into place and repeat with the back side of the tote, placing adhesive between the two layers right along the top edges. Pin in place. Make sure that the fusible adhesive tape is applied all the way around the top edge of the bag and then iron the layers together.

23. For each eyelet that you attach, you will need an eyelet front (taller barrel, *a*), an eyelet back (shorter barrel, *b*), a hammer plate (*c*), and a hammer post (*d*).

24. Lay your bag in front of you, with the open side at the top. Measure in from the right side seam 4 inches and 1 inch from the top, and make a mark with your pen. Do the same thing on the left side. Repeat with the back side of the bag.

25. Center an eyelet back over one of the dots and use it as a template to trace around the inside edge of the barrel. Repeat with the other three markings.

26. Cut out one of the circles with scissors.

27. Place the eyelet front through the hole from the outside of the tote.

28. Place the tote facedown onto your work surface and then place the eyelet back over the back of the eyelet front, which is on the inside of the tote. Place the hammer plate below the eyelet front. Place the hammer post on top of the eyelet back.

29. Tap the hammer post a few times with a regular hammer, until both eyelet pieces compress and pinch the fabric in between nice and tight. Repeat steps 26 through 29 with the other three traced circles.

30. Place one of your handle pieces in front of you, right side down. Fold each long edge over ½ inch toward the middle of the wrong side of the fabric and iron flat.

31. Fold one of the short ends over ¼ inch toward the wrong side of the fabric as well. Place a piece of ¼-inch-wide fusible adhesive tape under the flap and iron it down to activate the adhesive. Repeat with the other short end.

32. Fold the strip in half lengthwise, wrong sides together. Press flat. Open it up and slide two strips of ½-inch-wide fusible adhesive tape between the two folded layers; one goes along the center fold and the other between the two folded sides that are pressed together. Close it up again and iron flat to activate the adhesive. Repeat steps 30 through 32 with the other handle piece.

33. Bunch up one end of one of your straps and thread it through one of the eyelets at the front of the bag, coming from the inside of the bag and then out the front.

34. Tie a knot close to the very end of the strap and pull snug. Thread the other end of the strap through the other eyelet at the front of the bag. Tie a knot in this end as well. Repeat with the other strap along the back side of the bag.

35. If desired, create a Fabric Flower (page 107) and attach it to the front of the bag with some epoxy glue.

1

2

3

4

5

6

7

8

9

10

11

12

13

14

15

16

17

18

19

20

21

22

c   d

a   b

23

24

25

26

27

28

29

30

31

32

33

34

35

FABRIC WRISTLET KEY FOB

Whip up a key fob for yourself and everyone you know . . . and they'll thank you for making their keys easier to find, freeing up their busy hands, and creating an easier way to hang their keys while not in use.

SKILL LEVEL: I » TIME ESTIMATE: 30 MINUTES

Supplies

- ⅛ yard light- to medium-weight cotton fabric
- Double-sided fusible adhesive tape, ½ inch wide
- Key fob hardware (with key ring), 1¼ inches wide

Toolkit

- Scissors
- Measuring tape
- Iron/ironing board
- Hammer

1. Cut a piece of fabric that is 4½ x 12 inches. Fold the strip of fabric in half lengthwise, wrong sides together. Iron flat.

2. Open up the fabric and fold both long edges in toward the center fold.

3. Iron both new folds flat.

4. Fold it in half again along the original ironed fold, and iron one more time.

5. Open it up again and place two strips of fusible adhesive tape along one side of the fabric, placing them side by side. Fold the fabric closed again, sandwiching the adhesive between the fold. Iron to activate the adhesive according to the adhesive's package instructions. Avoid pulling or dragging the iron across the fabric.

6. Fold the long strip in half, lining up the two raw ends. Place the two ends inside the teeth of your key fob hardware.

7. Hammer the hardware closed, catching the fabric in between the metal teeth.

8. Attach the key ring.

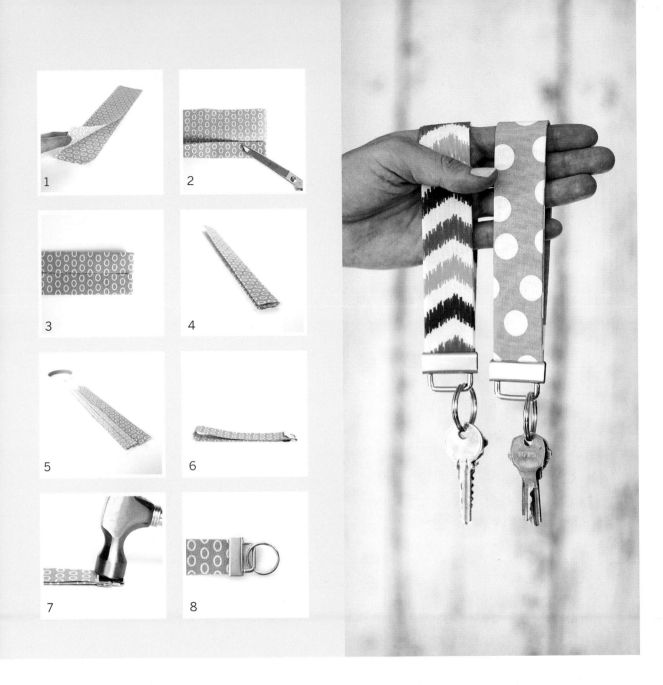

Tips!

You can lengthen the key fob (to wear around your neck) by lengthening the 12-inch measurement of fabric to about 36 inches (or more).

BUSINESS CARD HOLDER

It's always nice to have a particular home for your business cards, so they're ready at any moment. However, if you don't have your own business cards, you could use this to house a few credit cards while out shopping or as a spot for the seventeen random business cards that are filling up your junk drawer!

SKILL LEVEL: I » TIME ESTIMATE: 45 MINUTES

Supplies

- Piece of scrap leather, at least 6 x 8 inches
- Epoxy glue
- Flower template (page 238, optional)

Toolkit

- Scissors
- Ruler
- Straight pins
- Pen or fine-tip marker
- Clothespins or a heavy book

1. Cut a piece of leather that is 4 x 7½ inches.

2. Lay the leather in front of you, right side down, and place a pin vertically at the top long edge of your rectangle of leather 2½ inches from the upper left corner. Place another pin 2½ inches from the upper right corner. The pins should now be 2½ inches from each other. Use a ruler and a pen or fine-tip marker to draw a diagonal line from each pin down to its closest lower corner.

3. Cut the excess leather away along the line. Apply a line of epoxy glue along the bottom edge of the leather on the right third (2½ inches long).

4. Fold the right side of the leather 2½ inches over to the left. Apply pressure while the glue dries completely. (Using clothespins or a heavy book will help with this.)

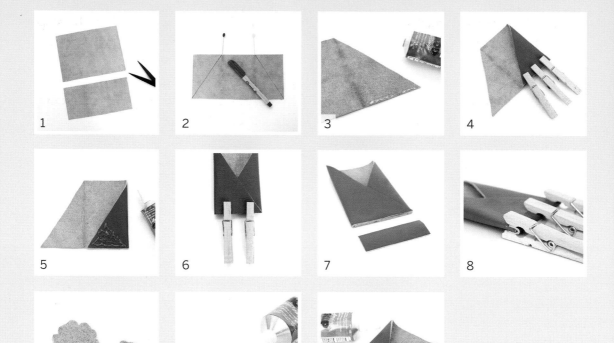

5. Add a line of glue along the left-most third of the bottom edge. You don't want glue to leak into the inside of the card holder, but you also don't want it to ooze out to the right side of the flap. (Before adding the glue, it will help to fold over the left flap and see where it will cover and apply glue accordingly.)

6. Fold the left flap over to the right and apply pressure while the glue dries completely. (Again, clothespins or a heavy book will help with this.)

7. Cut a piece of leather that is 1 x 2½ inches. (In case your folded business card is slightly wider or narrower than the 2½ inches that it should be, line up this narrow rectangle below the bottom edge of the card holder. It should be exactly the same width.)

8. Apply glue to the wrong side of this strip of leather and sandwich it securely around the bottom edge of the card holder, creating a nice finished edge. Pinch clothespins around the leather strip or place a book on top until the glue dries.

9. You can leave the card holder as is or add a little flower to the front if you have extra leather, using the template on page 238. Cut out two flowers of different sizes and a center circle piece.

10. Stack the flowers and center and glue them all together.

11. Glue the embellishment to the front of the card holder, making sure that none of the glue leaks onto the inside of the card holder.

Tips!

If you can't locate any leather, you can use vinyl (faux leather). Sometimes it can be a little trickier to manipulate, but keep at it—it will give in eventually!

If you don't like the idea of a flower on the front, consider cutting a plain circle and gluing that down in place of the flower. Then cut out an initial that represents the business and glue that on top of the circle. Or get creative and add any ol' thing you want to the front!

Chapter 4

CLOTHING

Be sure to read the Helpful Tips section (page 13) for washing and care instructions for clothing made with adhesives.

Use the sizing charts (pages 14–15) for reference, if needed.

BASIC SKIRT

Need something new to wear this weekend? Whip up a quick skirt in the color you've been trying to find to pair with those shoes you adore! Dress it up, dress it down . . . this skirt is perfect for any occasion and for girls and ladies of all ages.

SKILL LEVEL: II » **TIME ESTIMATE: 45 MINUTES**

Supplies

- 1–2 yards cotton fabric (more or less, depending on size)
- Double-sided fusible adhesive tape, ¼ inch wide and ½ inch wide
- Elastic, 1 inch wide (amount depends on waist measurement)

Toolkit

- Scissors
- Flexible measuring tape
- Ruler or hem guide ruler
- Iron/ironing board
- Pinking shears
- Safety pin

1. Measure your subject's waist and add 1 inch to get the fabric width measurement. Determine how long you'd like to make the skirt and add 3¾ inches; that's your fabric height measurement. Cut two pieces of fabric to those dimensions, making sure the patterns are going the same direction, if applicable.

2. Place the two pieces together, with the right sides of the fabric together, matching up the sides, tops, and bottoms. (The width of your fabric should run left to right.) Fold back the top piece of fabric a few inches along the left side of the skirt. Place a piece of ½-inch-wide fusible adhesive tape between the two layers, close to the cut edges and running the entire length. Fold the top piece back down, lining up the edges again. Iron in place according to the adhesive's package instructions. Avoid pulling or dragging the iron across the fabric. Repeat with the right side of the skirt, fusing the two edges together the same way. These are the two side seams of your skirt.

3. Trim the very edges of the fused layers with pinking shears, only barely trimming the edge of the adhesive. This will help keep the edges from fraying.

4. Turn your tube of fabric right side out and iron the fabric open where the two edges were fused together along both sides. Make sure to iron the excess fabric off to one side, down the entire length of the fabric.

5. Turn the tube of fabric inside out and lift up one of the side flaps of excess fabric and place a strip of ¼-inch-wide fusible adhesive tape under the flap, along the entire length.

6. Press the flap back down and iron in place, fusing the layers together. Repeat with the other flap of fabric along the other side of the skirt.

7. With the skirt still inside out, fold the bottom edge of the skirt up ½ inch and iron flat.

8. Fold it up another 1 inch and iron flat again.

9. Lift the folded edge and place a strip of ½-inch-wide fusible adhesive tape under it, lining it up with the upper folded edge, all the way around the bottom of the skirt.

10. Iron in place, fusing the layers together.

11. With the skirt still inside out, fold the upper edge of the skirt down ½ inch and iron flat.

12. Fold it down another 1¾ inches and iron flat.

13. Lift the folded edge and place a piece of ½-inch-wide fusible adhesive tape under it, right near the edge. Attach the adhesive all the way around the skirt, leaving a 2-inch gap along the back (to insert the elastic). Iron in place.

14. Cut a piece of elastic to the waist measurement of your subject, plus 1 inch. Attach a safety pin to one end of the elastic and insert that through the opening of the casing you just created.

15. Push the elastic through the casing bit by bit until you've threaded it all the way around the waist. Be careful not to let the elastic get twisted.

16. Remove the safety pin and overlap the two elastic ends by 2 inches.

17. Place two rows of ½-inch-wide fusible adhesive tape side by side between the two layers of overlapped elastic ends. Iron the layers to activate the adhesive.

18. Manipulate the fused elastic ends back into the casing and then add a strip of ½-inch-wide fusible adhesive tape between the layers of the fabric opening to finish off the casing.

19. Iron it closed to activate the adhesive.

20. Evenly distribute the elastic through-out the casing and then gently steam the gathers to keep them in place a little better. (Don't iron them flat, as it will create severe creases. Just gently steam them so that they lie a little flatter.)

Tips!

You can use these directions to make this skirt for tiny tots all the way to grown adults . . . it works the same!

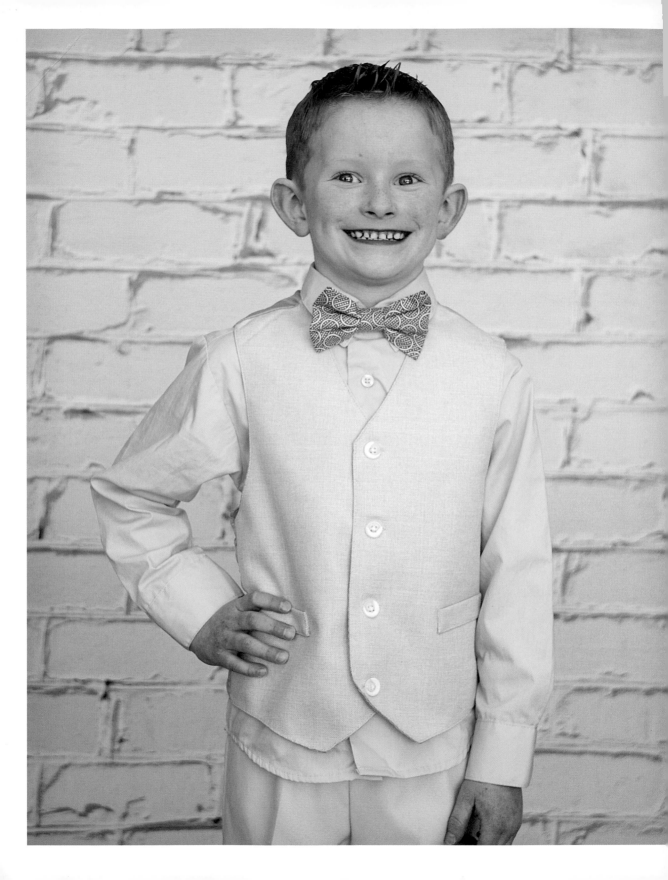

LITTLE BOY'S BOW TIE

What's cuter than a little boy in a mini bow tie? Not much. Bow ties are perfect for special occasions or just to add some fun to any outfit. And by making them adjustable, they'll grow with your little guy as he struts his stuff for years to come!

SKILL LEVEL: II » TIME ESTIMATE: 60 MINUTES

Supplies

- ¼ yard lightweight cotton fabric
- Double-sided fusible adhesive tape, ½ inch wide
- Epoxy glue
- Bow tie hardware set, ¾ inch wide

Toolkit

- Scissors
- Ruler
- Straight pins
- Iron/ironing board
- Clothespin

This bow tie is made to fit sizes 2T to 8 years old. The finished size of the actual bow is about 4 inches wide and 2½ inches tall, at its tallest point.

1. Cut a piece of fabric that measures 6½ x 8½ inches. Fold the two long sides toward the center, wrong sides together, overlapping them by ½ inch (making the fabric about 3 inches wide). Press flat with your iron.

2. Lift up the top flap of fabric and place a strip of fusible adhesive tape along the underside of the upper edge. Fold it closed again and iron flat according to the adhesive's package instructions. Avoid pulling or dragging the iron across the fabric.

3. Fold both raw ends toward the center, overlapping them by ½ inch (making the fabric about 4 inches wide).

4. Lift up the top flap of fabric and place a strip of fusible adhesive tape along the underside of this top flap, next to the raw edge. Fold it closed again and iron flat to fuse the layers together. Set aside.

5. Cut another piece of fabric that measures 1½ x 3 inches. Fold both 3-inch-long sides over ¾ inch toward the center, wrong sides together.

6. Open the flaps and place a piece of fusible adhesive tape down the center of the fabric, along the entire length where the flaps meet when closed. Place the flaps back down and iron flat, activating the adhesive. Set aside.

7. Grab the bigger piece of fabric that you finished folding in step 4 and hold it in front of you lengthwise, with the fused ends facing away from you. Make little accordion folds along the center of the fabric and pinch it between your thumb and finger, creating a bow shape.

8. Place a blob of epoxy glue at the center, right on top of the folds you just created.

9. Place the center of the smaller strip that you created in steps 5 and 6 with the folded edges facedown onto the glue and perpendicular to the bow width.

10. Wrap the two ends of the strip around the center of the bow and pull firmly toward the back side of the bow. Pinch the two ends together with a clothespin until the glue dries.

11. For one bow tie, you will need a hook (a), loop (b), and slide adjuster (c).

12. Cut another piece of fabric 17 x 2½ inches, for the neck strap. Fold it in half lengthwise with the wrong sides together and iron flat.

13. Open it back up and fold both long sides toward the ironed crease. Iron flat.

14. Fold in half again along the original fold from step 12 and iron flat. Open the strip again and place a piece of fusible adhesive tape between the two folds that extends all the way down the strip. Fold closed again and iron flat to activate the adhesive. The strip should now be about ⅝ inch wide.

15. Thread one end of your fabric strip through the opening of the loop piece. Fold the end over by 1½ inches.

16. Fold the raw edge under ½ inch.

17. Lift up the folded edge very carefully as you add some adhesive to the underside of the fold, making sure to keep your folds in place.

18. Fold it back down and iron in place to activate the adhesive.

19. Place the neck strap in front of you horizontally, front side facing up. Orient the loop hardware piece at the left and the raw end of the strip at the right. Thread your slide adjuster onto the right end of your fabric strip (use the photo for reference).

20. Scoot the slide adjuster down the strip of fabric, creating a loop of fabric coming out the top of the slider.

21. Slide the hook onto the right end of the fabric strip, orienting the hook as shown in the photo.

22. Don't move any of the hardware but lay the fabric down on its side, positioning it as shown in the photo.

23. Take the raw end of your fabric strip and loop it around and into the right slot of the slide adjuster.

24. Pull the end through the slide adjuster an inch or two and then fold it back into the left slot of the slide adjuster.

25. Pull and adjust the fabric strip so that you have enough slack at the end of your fabric to now fold it under ½ inch and pin in place. Cut a ½-inch-long piece of fusible adhesive tape, remove the pin, and place the adhesive under the fold. Pin in place again. Without disturbing the pinned fold, slide the hardware away from this end as much as possible to give some room for ironing.

26. Iron flat to activate the ½-inch section of adhesive.

27. Adjust the hardware and hook it together to be sure it functions properly.

28. Unhook the hardware and place the front side of the neck strap onto the back side of the bow tie. Wrap the ends of the center bow strip around the neck strap and glue one end down first. Then fold the other end down, tucking the raw ends under enough so that the fold is centered on the back of the bow. Glue in place and hold firmly until dry.

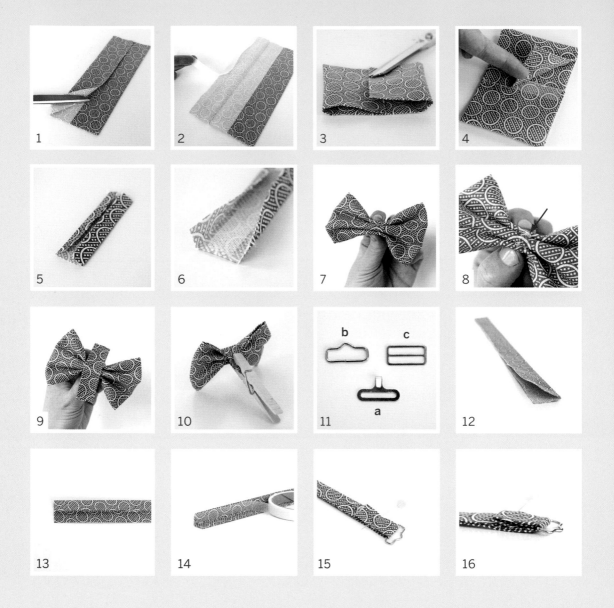

1

2

3

4

5

6

7

8

9

10

11

12

13

14

15

16

17   18   19   20

21   22   23   24

25   26   27   28

Tips!

When gluing the neck strap to the back of the bow, be sure to leave enough room on the side of the strap with the slide adjuster so that you have plenty of room to adjust the size of the bow tie.

Bow tie hardware (or something similar) can usually be found at larger fabric stores, but there's a wider selection online.

INFINITY SCARF

Ahh, the infinity scarf. Such a great little accessory to turn that plain outfit into something darling! Wear it long, loop it around twice, or intertwine it with another color. It's nice and simple and perfect all year long.

SKILL LEVEL: I » TIME ESTIMATE: 45 MINUTES

Supplies

- 2 yards lightweight cotton fabric (something sheer like voile works great)
- Double-sided fusible adhesive tape, ¼ inch wide and ½ inch wide

Toolkit

- Scissors
- Measuring tape
- Ruler or hem guide ruler
- Iron/ironing board

The finished scarf measures 21 x 62 inches.

1. Cut a large rectangle of fabric that measures 22 x 65 inches.

2. With the wrong side up, fold over one of the long edges ½ inch toward the wrong side. Iron flat. Fold it over again, another ½ inch toward the wrong side, and iron flat.

3. Lift up the top fold and place a piece of ¼-inch-wide fusible adhesive tape along the entire length of the folded edge. Press this fold back down and iron it in place according to the adhesive's package instructions. Avoid pulling or dragging the iron across the fabric. Repeat with the other long edge and iron to activate the adhesive.

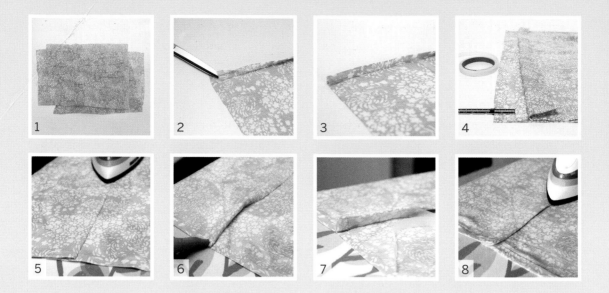

Tips!

The reason two adhesive widths are used in this project is that adhesive will stiffen up the fabric, and you want to keep that to a minimum around the circumference of the scarf. If you prefer not to purchase two widths, the best solution is to purchase the ¼ inch and then use two strips of it side by side when needed, rather than buying the ½ inch and cutting it in half. It's easier to have a nice straight edge when using the fusible adhesive tape on projects, and cutting it can be a bit frustrating to keep even.

4. Fold your scarf in half widthwise (right sides together) and match up the raw edges of your two ends. Fold back the raw edge of the top half a few inches. Measure in 1½ inches from the raw edge of the bottom piece of fabric and place a line of ½-inch-wide fusible adhesive tape 1½ inches in from (and parallel to) the raw edge. Fold the top raw edge back down into place and match up both raw ends again. Iron in place, fusing the layers together.

5. Turn your newly constructed tube right side out. Slip the tube over the ironing board and iron where the two ends are joined, ironing the joined ends flat and off to one side.

6. Turn the tube inside-out and slip it back over the ironing board, with the wrong side facing up. Fold the raw edges under ½ inch and iron flat.

7. Lift up the top fold and place a piece of ½-inch-wide fusible adhesive tape along the folded edge, reaching from one side of the scarf all the way to the other.

8. Press this fold back down and iron it in place, activating the adhesive.

HALF APRON

Are you in need of a handy apron to throw on while baking, crafting, or cleaning so you don't have to worry about where you're going to wipe those messy hands and fingers? Well, look no more, because this super-simple apron will fix that problem right up for you.

SKILL LEVEL: I » TIME ESTIMATE: 45 MINUTES

Supplies

- ¾ yard medium-weight cotton fabric
- Double-sided fusible adhesive tape, ½ inch wide
- 3 yards grosgrain ribbon, 1½ inches wide

Toolkit

- Scissors
- Measuring tape
- Ruler or hem guide ruler
- Iron/ironing board
- Pen or fine-tip marker

1. Cut a piece of fabric that measures 25 x 22 inches. Fold over one of your 22-inch edges ½ inch toward the wrong side of the fabric and iron it flat. Fold it over another ½ inch and iron again.

2. Lift up the top fold and place a piece of fusible adhesive tape along the entire length of the folded edge. Press this fold back down and iron it in place according to the adhesive's package instructions. Avoid pulling or dragging the iron across the fabric. Repeat with the other 22-inch side.

3. Flip the fabric over and orient the pattern to find the top and bottom (if applicable), with the two short edges on the sides. Turn the fabric wrong side up and fold the bottom edge over ½ inch toward the wrong side of the fabric and iron it flat. Fold it over another ½ inch and iron flat.

4. Place adhesive under the fold and iron it to activate the adhesive.

5. Fold the top edge down ½ inch toward the wrong side of the fabric and iron flat.

6. Fold the top down again 1½ inches. Iron flat.

7. Lift up the folded edge and place three strips of fusible adhesive tape side by side along the entire length of the edge (making one big strip of adhesive, 1½ inches wide), right up against the fold. (Be sure that once you fold that flap of fabric back down, the adhesive will be completely covered.) Mark the center of the upper edge of the apron and the center of your long piece of ribbon. Place your ribbon right on top of the adhesive, matching up the middle of the ribbon with the center of the top edge of the apron. The ribbon should cover the fusible adhesive tape.

8. Place three more strips of fusible adhesive tape the width of the apron side by side on top of the ribbon.

9. Fold the flap of fabric down on top of this layer of fusible adhesive tape, hiding the ribbon and adhesive completely, and then iron it flat, activating the adhesive.

Tips!

If you'd like to make the apron bigger or smaller, go for it! That's the nice thing about making things from scratch: you decide! This finished apron is 23 x 19 inches. Adjust accordingly.

While attaching the ribbon to the top edge of the apron, be patient as you're ironing all of those layers together. It may take more time for the adhesive to heat up and adhere to the fabric.

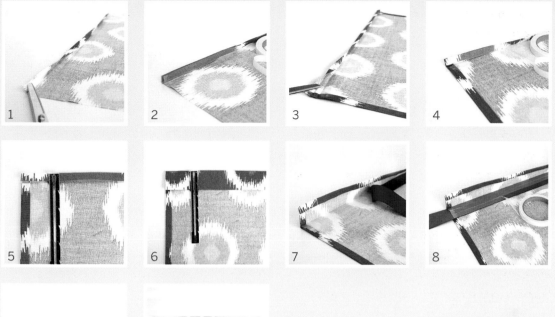

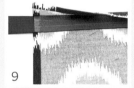

FLUFFY TUTU

For some reason, once your little girl steps into a full and fluffy tutu, the magic of twirling, spinning, and leaping across the floor begins immediately. However, tutus aren't just for little girls: the magic works equally well for girls of all ages. Promise.

SKILL LEVEL: I » TIME ESTIMATE: 90 MINUTES

Supplies

- 5–6 yards tulle
- Cord elastic (amount depends on waist measurement)

Toolkit

- Scissors
- Flexible measuring tape

1. Cut the tulle into 2-inch-wide pieces. To get the length measurement of the strips, determine the length you'd like the tutu to be and then double that number and add 2 inches. (For example, if you want a 10-inch-long tutu, cut strips that are 22 inches long and 2 inches wide.) To save time while cutting, cut through several layers of tulle at once.

2. Measure the waist of your subject and cut a piece of elastic that's the same length as the waist plus 1 inch. Knot the two ends of elastic together, leaving an inch free at each end. Slide the elastic around the back of a chair.

3. Working with two overlapped strips of tulle at a time, fold them in half. Slide the folded end behind the elastic from the top.

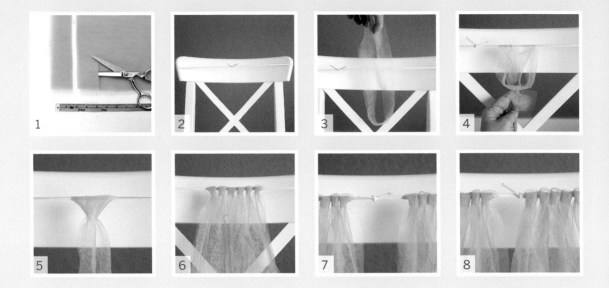

4. Pull the free ends down around the elastic and through the loop of tulle, tightening up the knot just a bit.

5. Continue pulling gently downward, creating a neat knot around the elastic.

6. Repeat with more strips of tulle all the way around the elastic.

7. Once you make it all the way around, be sure that the tutu fits correctly and then pull the elastic knot nice and snug.

8. Attach a few more strips of tulle onto the elastic band, covering the elastic ends beneath the knots of tulle.

Tips!

The tulle yardage recommended above is for little girls ages 2 to 6. Add another couple yards or so for older children and adult sizes.

If your tutu isn't fluffy enough, add more strips of tulle. Easy as that!

If you're unsure how the tutu will fit, add a few inches to the elastic waistband and only tie it loosely. Re-size it after all the tulle is attached for a custom fit.

KNIT SKIRT WITH SASH

Some girls love skirts and need one of every shape and variety. This skirt with a sash will not disappoint skirt lovers big and small. It's made of a comfy knit, it has plenty of movement, and the little sash adds such a darling detail. This skirt may well become the new favorite!

SKILL LEVEL: II » **TIME ESTIMATE: 90 MINUTES**

Supplies

- ½ yard or more jersey knit fabric (amount depends on size)
- Elastic, 1½ inches wide (length depends on size)
- Double-sided fusible adhesive tape, ½ inch wide

Toolkit

- Scissors
- Straight pins
- Flexible measuring tape
- Ruler or hem guide ruler
- Iron/ironing board
- Safety pin

1. Measure the waist of your subject. Add 1 inch to that number for the width of your fabric piece. For the length, decide on the desired length of the skirt and then add 2¼ inches to that measurement. Cut two pieces of jersey knit to those specifications. For the sash, you will need two strips that are 4 inches wide. For the length measurement of each sash, multiply the waist measurement by 1½. Cut two sash pieces to those specifications from the jersey knit. (For example, if you are making a skirt for a girl who has a 20-inch waist and wants the skirt to be 12 inches long, you would cut out two main pieces that are 21 x 14¼ inches and two sash strips that are 4 x 30 inches.)

2. Place one of your sash pieces with the wrong side facing up and lay a 4-inch-long piece of fusible adhesive tape on the edge of a short end.

3. While keeping the fusible adhesive tape in place, fold the long sides of the sash in

toward the wrong side of the fabric, until they meet in the middle.

4. Press with an iron to activate the adhesive according to the adhesive's package instructions. Avoid pulling or dragging the iron across the fabric. Repeat with one end of the other sash strip and another piece of fusible adhesive tape.

5. Place one of your skirt pieces in front of you with the right side facing up. Then place one sash piece right side up across the top of the skirt and line the folded and fused end up with the edge of the skirt piece, 2¼ inches from the top. Repeat on the other side with the second sash piece.

6. Without disturbing the placement of the sash, fold back the fused and folded end of one of the sash pieces and place two strips of the fusible adhesive tape side by side, right next to the skirt edge and cut to the width of the sash piece. Lay the sash end back down and iron in place to activate the adhesive. Repeat with the second sash piece on the other side of the skirt piece.

7. Place the other skirt piece facedown on top of the first piece (right sides of the fabric together) and match up all the sides. Without disturbing the placement of the

skirt pieces, fold back the side edge of the piece on top, just a few inches. Then lay a long piece of fusible adhesive tape along the very side edge of the bottom piece. (Be sure that the two sash pieces are out of the way.) Fold the top skirt piece back in place and line up the side edges again. Press with an iron to activate the adhesive. (Lift and press as you iron; don't drag and pull.) Repeat along the other side edge. Take a peek at your adhered edges and be sure that the adhesive has melted and secured the fabric together properly.

8. Turn the skirt right side out and then press open the side seams you just created, folding the excess fabric flaps on the inside of the skirt toward the back of the skirt.

9. Turn the skirt inside out and then fold over the top edge of the skirt 2¼ inches. Pin in place.

10. On the back side of the skirt, remove a few pins from the center. Lift up the unpinned flap of fabric just a bit and begin placing a continuous piece of fusible adhesive tape along the wrong side of the skirt, right where the bottom edge of the folded-over portion would cover it. After folding the fabric back down, you want the fusible adhesive tape to sit on the very bottom edge of the folded-over fabric so that after it's ironed in place, there will still be a casing wide enough for your 1½-inch-wide elastic to slide through. Re-pin this section. (Be sure to pin through the fusible adhesive tape to hold it in place as well.)

11. Continue all the way around the top of the skirt, unpinning a small section at a time to lay the long piece of fusible adhesive tape down. Stop a few inches before you make it all the way around (to leave an opening to insert the elastic) and cut off the fusible adhesive tape. Iron all the way around the skirt (removing pins as you go) to activate the adhesive. Once you're done, your casing will be in place, with a nice gap in the back.

12. Cut a piece of elastic that is 1 inch longer than the waist measurement and attach a safety pin to one end. Thread the elastic all the way around the inside of the casing and pull the safety pin out the other end. Make sure that you have both ends sticking out and that your elastic isn't twisted inside the casing.

13. Remove the safety pin and overlap the ends of the elastic by 2 inches. Place a few strips of fusible adhesive tape side by side between the two layers where the ends overlap. Iron together to activate the adhesive.

14. Place a strip of fusible adhesive tape that is just long enough to fill the bottom edge of the gap in the fabric casing. Iron the opening closed to activate the adhesive. Be sure to check all of your ironed seams to see that the adhesive was heated up properly.

15. Adjust the elastic so that it is evenly distributed throughout the casing. Turn your skirt right side out and then tie your sash ends into a bow. (Cut off any excess sash length.)

Tips!

The cool thing about knit fabric is that it doesn't fray, so you can leave the bottom edge of the skirt and the sash ends unhemmed. However, if you prefer to finish off the bottom hem of this skirt, add a little extra to your fabric length and adjust accordingly (just like the Basic Skirt on page 130).

GRAPHIC T-SHIRT

Turn your artwork designs into something that can be worn by kids or adults for team events, family reunions, or other activities. Freezer paper is wax coated on one side and shiny and smooth to the touch. Once heated, the waxy side adheres very slightly to whatever it's touching but will come off completely once it's pulled away. Create any design you want and then mix colors, add different layers, insert names, or anything else you can dream up.

SKILL LEVEL: III »   **TIME ESTIMATE: 60 MINUTES**

Supplies

- Paper airplane template (page 239, optional)
- Printer
- Freezer paper
- Scrap piece of cardboard
- Fabric paint
- Blunt-edge paintbrush

Toolkit

- Scissors
- Iron/ironing board
- Utility knife
- Cutting mat
- Pencil

1. Create the image you'll use by either drawing it (by hand or using a computer program) or finding an image on the computer that you like and placing it in a document that you can then print. Add text if you like, size it to fit the shirt, then print. (If you're using the paper airplane template, enlarge it to the size needed for your shirt.) Tape your image to a window during daylight.

2. Tape a similarly sized piece of freezer paper over the top of your image with the shiny side facing the image.

3. Trace your image, drawing right onto the paper side of the freezer paper.

4. Cut out your image with a sharp utility knife, piece by piece, starting with the innermost shapes first.

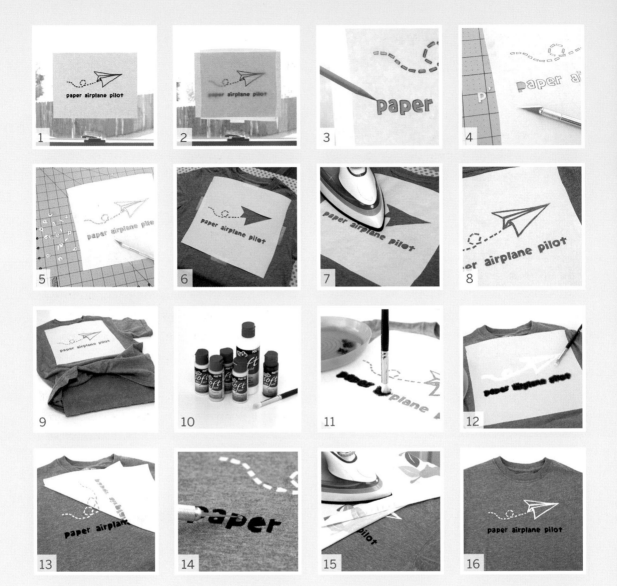

Tips!

The fabric paint used on your shirt is machine washable and dryable.

5. You will need the negative space pieces, so don't throw those small pieces away.

6. Once all your pieces are cut out, lay the freezer paper down on the shirt (shiny side facing down onto the shirt) and center it just where you'd like it. (Taping down the edges while you find a good placement can be really helpful.)

7. Turn your iron on to medium heat and begin pressing the freezer paper onto the shirt. Make sure to iron around the tape pieces (if you used them) and then remove them completely once the freezer paper has begun to adhere to the shirt. (If you try to lift the freezer paper with your fingernail, it should stay in place. If it doesn't, iron again. However, if you use an iron that is too hot or if you iron for too long, the wax finish may melt off completely and you'll have to re-cut your image. So be careful and work slowly.)

8. Grab the negative space pieces and fit them into the design, to make the image complete. Iron in place.

9. Carefully slide the scrap of cardboard between the two layers of T-shirt, making sure that it's larger than the image area where you'll be painting.

10. Select a fabric paint color.

11. Start with small amounts of paint on your paintbrush tip and dab it into the open area of your image. You don't want to overwhelm the area with paint or cause it to leak, so start with a little bit of paint and reapply as needed.

12. You may want to switch colors, but if they overlap at all, make sure the first layer dries completely and then proceed.

13. Allow all of the paint to dry completely. (Using a hairdryer to help speed up the process works really well.) Then peel the freezer paper away from the shirt.

14. The tiny pieces that were ironed on will need a little extra help. Use the pointy tip of your utility knife to pry up an edge and then peel.

15. Use a thin towel or piece of fabric to cover your painted area while you apply heat over it with an iron. This will help set the paint, making it permanent.

16. Admire and enjoy.

LITTLE GIRL'S RIBBON DRESS

Maybe you have a little girl who's obsessed with dresses (like mine is!). If so, add another to her collection that's comfy, breezy, and perfect for the warmer months. Oh, and those little ribbons tied together into bows at the shoulder? Love.

SKILL LEVEL: II » **TIME ESTIMATE: 90 MINUTES**

Supplies

- 1–2 yards lightweight cotton fabric (more or less, depending on size)
- Double-sided fusible adhesive tape, ¼ inch wide and ½ inch wide
- Elastic, 1 inch wide (length depends on size)
- 4 (¼-inch) metal eyelet sets
- Eyelet setter hammer tool (or other eyelet tool)
- 6–7 feet ribbon, ¾–1 inch wide

Toolkit

- Scissors
- Flexible measuring tape
- Ruler or hem guide ruler
- Iron/ironing board
- Pinking shears
- Hammer
- Lighter
- Straight pins
- Pen or fine-tip marker
- Safety pin

1. Measure the chest circumference of your subject. Multiply that number by 2 to get the width dimension. Measure from the top of the chest of your subject (at the arm pit) down to the desired length and add 4½ inches to get the height dimension. Cut a piece of fabric to those dimensions.

2. Fold your fabric in half widthwise with right sides together, matching up the two shorter ends.

3. Place a piece of ½-inch-wide fusible adhesive tape between the two layers, right up against the side edges. Iron to fuse the layers together according to the adhesive's package instructions. Avoid pulling or dragging the iron across the fabric.

4. Trim the very edge of the fused layers with pinking shears (only slightly cutting through the adhesive), which will keep this edge from fraying.

5. Open up the fabric to the right side and iron the fabric open where the two ends were fused together. Iron the flap of excess fabric on the other side over to one side. Turn the dress inside out again.

6. Lift up the flap of fabric and place a strip of ¼-inch-wide adhesive under the flap.

7. Press the flap back down and iron in place to activate your adhesive.

8. With your fabric still inside out, fold the bottom edge of the dress up ½ inch and iron flat.

9. Fold the bottom edge up another inch and iron flat again.

10. Lift the edge back up and place a strip of ½-inch-wide fusible adhesive tape under the fold, lining it up with the upper folded edge, all the way around the bottom of the dress.

11. Iron in place to activate the adhesive.

12. With the dress still inside out, fold the upper edge of the dress down ½ inch and iron flat. Fold it down again another 2½ inches and iron flat.

13. Lift up the flap of fabric and place a piece of ½-inch-wide adhesive tape along the second fold, along the very top of the dress, all the way around the dress.

Iron flat, making sure the adhesive stays in the top part of the fold.

14. Lift the flap again and add another strip of fusible adhesive tape, lined up with the edge of the bottom of the fold. There will be about 1½ inches between the two strips of adhesive, which will serve as a casing for your elastic.

15. Attach the adhesive all the way around the dress, leaving a 2-inch gap along the back (to insert the elastic). Iron flat to activate the adhesive, making sure the adhesive stays lined up with the very bottom of the fold without sneaking out beneath.

16. Cut a piece of elastic to the length of the upper chest measurement of your subject, plus 1 inch. Attach a safety pin to one end of the elastic and insert it through the opening of the casing you just created.

17. Push the safety pin through the casing bit by bit, pulling the elastic right along with it, until you make your way through the entire casing.

18. Make sure the elastic hasn't twisted, remove the safety pin, and overlap the two elastic ends by 2 inches.

19. Place two rows of ½-inch-wide fusible adhesive tape side by side between the two layers of overlapped elastic. Iron the layers to activate the adhesive.

20. Manipulate the fused elastic ends back into the casing and then add a strip of ½-inch-wide fusible adhesive tape to the lower fold of the opening. Iron it closed to activate the adhesive.

21. Evenly distribute the elastic throughout the casing and then gently steam the gathers to keep them in place a little better. (Don't iron them flat, which will add severe creases, just gently steam them so they lie a little flatter.)

22. With the vertical seam along the center back, lay the dress down in front of you. Place a pin at the exact center in the front and then two more pins dividing each half in half, marking the dress front in even quarters. The side pins will be where your straps attach at the front. Place two pins along the back side of the dress, directly behind the two side pins, marking where your straps will attach in the back.

23. For each eyelet that you attach, you will need an eyelet front (taller barrel, a), an eyelet back (shorter barrel, b), a hammer plate (c), and a hammer post (d).

24. Where each of your straps is marked with a pin, use the eyelet back as a template to draw a circle where your eyelet will be attached. Mark each circle about ¼ inch from the top edge of the dress, without hitting the elastic band.

25. Cut out each circle with scissors.

26. Place the eyelet front through the hole from the right side of the dress.

27. Place the eyelet back over the back of the eyelet front, which is on the inside of the dress. Place the hammer plate below the eyelet front, on the right side of the dress.

28. Place the hammer post on top of the eyelet back and tap it a few times with a regular hammer, until both eyelet pieces compress and pinch the fabric in between nice and tight.

29. Repeat with the remaining eyelet locations.

30. Cut four pieces of ribbon, each about 20 inches long, more or less, depending on your subject's size and preference. Carefully heat-seal the cut ends with a lighter to melt them and keep them from fraying.

31. Thread one end of one of the pieces of ribbon through one of the eyelets, entering from the right side of the dress. Fold the end of the ribbon over, wrong sides together, about 2 inches. Place a few pieces of ½-inch-wide fusible adhesive tape between the overlapped layers of ribbon.

32. Iron the ribbon to activate the adhesive. Repeat with the other three pieces of ribbon.

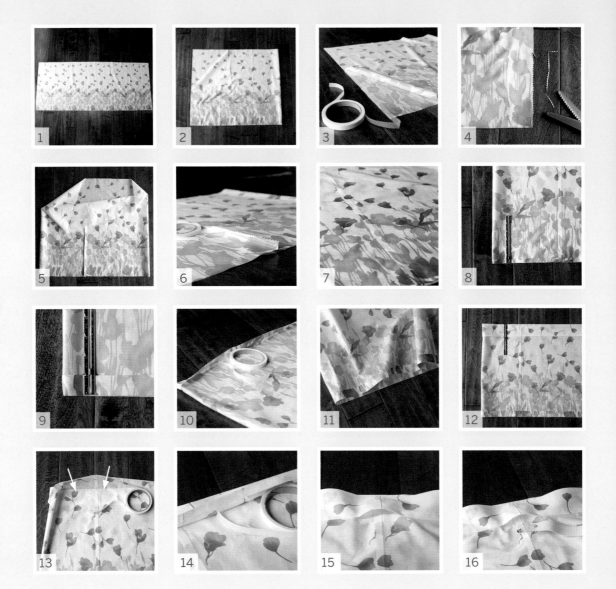

17

18

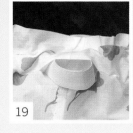

19

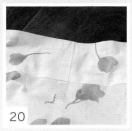

20

21

22

23

24

25

26

27

28

29

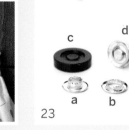

30

31

32

FRINGE SCARF

Turn a boring outfit into something a little more sassy and fun with this breathable knit scarf. You can wear this lightweight scarf at any time of year!

SKILL LEVEL: 1 » TIME ESTIMATE: 15 MINUTES

Supplies

- 2 yards jersey knit fabric

Toolkit

- Scissors
- Measuring tape

1. Cut your piece of knit down to 15 x 72 inches.

2. Fold your strip in half lengthwise.

3. Starting 1 inch from an end, make 6½-inch-long cuts along the folded edge, spacing each cut about 1 inch apart.

4. Continue all the way down the length of the folded strip, stopping about an inch from the other end.

5. Open up the fabric and you'll see a bunch of slits along your scarf.

Tips!

There are different types of jersey knit. Some are more stretchy and slinky than others. Some have an equal stretch both left to right and top to bottom, while others stretch more in one direction than the other. This variation in knit fabrics may give your scarf a different look, but don't worry—any jersey knit will look great!

If your cuts aren't completely even or they vary slightly in width, don't stress! You'll never even notice once the scarf is on.

While cutting, be sure to keep the edges lined up so that the fabric doesn't shift and create uneven strips at the end.

Try folding the scarf in half lengthwise and then wrap it around your neck, letting all the fringes hang in separate folded pieces. Or open it up completely, revealing all the slits, and wrap it around your neck for a different look.

1

2

3

4

5

Chapter 5

HOLIDAY

VALENTINE TABLECLOTH

Create a whimsical Valentine holiday spread with this simple stenciled heart tablecloth. The design is so sweet and universal that you'll find yourself pulling this out for birthdays and other special occasions as well.

Supplies

- 5 yards lightweight cotton woven fabric
- Double-sided fusible adhesive tape, ¼ inch wide and ½ inch wide
- Freezer paper
- Heart template (page 240)
- Scrap piece of cardboard
- Sponge or sponge brush
- Fabric paint
- Paper plate

Toolkit

- Scissors
- Pinking shears
- Measuring tape
- Ruler or hem guide ruler
- Iron/ironing board
- Utility knife
- Cutting mat
- Pen or pencil

The finished tablecloth measures approximately 85 x 60 inches.

1. Cut two pieces from your fabric that are 87 x 31½ inches. Lay them right sides together, matching up the sides and ends evenly. Along one of the long sides, lift up and fold back the edge of the top piece of fabric and place a strip of ½-inch-wide fusible adhesive tape along the edge of the bottom piece. Return the top piece of fabric back over the bottom fabric and line up the edges again. Iron to activate the adhesive according to the adhesive's package instructions. Avoid pulling or dragging the iron across the fabric.

2. Trim the very edge of the fused layers with pinking shears (only slightly cutting through the adhesive), which will keep this edge from fraying.

3. Open up the fabric to the right side and iron the fabric open where the two ends were fused together. Turn the tablecloth over to the wrong side and iron again, making sure that the flap of fabric is flat and off to one side, down the entire length.

4. Place a strip of ¼-inch-wide fusible adhesive tape beneath the flap, along the entire length. Press the flap back down and iron in place to activate the adhesive. Now you have one big piece of fabric to use as your tablecloth.

5. Along one of the long sides, fold over the edge ½ inch toward the wrong side of the fabric and iron it flat. Fold it over another ½ inch and iron again.

6. Lift the folded edge back up and place a strip of ½-inch-wide fusible adhesive tape along the upper folded edge, all the way across the long edge of folded fabric.

7. Fold the flap of fabric back down and iron in place to activate the adhesive. Repeat with the other long side.

8. Repeat steps 5 through 7 with the two shorter ends, completing the edges all the way around your tablecloth.

9. Cut a piece of freezer paper that is 75 x 10 inches. Use the template or create your own 5½-inch heart shape and cut it out from any type of scrap paper. Trace the heart onto the strip of freezer paper several times (on the paper side, not the shiny side), spacing them about 4 inches apart and about 1½ inches from the bottom edge of the freezer paper. (You should be able to fit seven or so hearts along your strip of freezer paper, depending on how many hearts you'd like along your tablecloth.)

10. Cut out each heart from your strip of freezer paper.

11. Place your strip of heart cutouts, with the shiny side facedown onto the right side of your fabric, on one of the long sides. Line up the bottom edge of the paper with the bottom edge of your fabric and center it on both ends.

12. Iron your freezer paper onto the fabric on medium-low heat, only ironing long enough to adhere the paper to the fabric. (If you iron too long or the iron is too hot, the adhesive on the freezer paper will melt completely and you'll have to re-cut from new paper.)

13. Place a piece of cardboard under the fabric to protect your work surface from any paint that might bleed through. Dip your sponge (or sponge brush) into some fabric paint and blot out the excess on a paper plate.

14. Dab your sponge onto the fabric inside each heart cutout, creating a textured look. Reapply the paint as needed.

15. Let the paint dry completely (a hairdryer can help speed this up) and then peel the freezer paper off the fabric.

16. Place a thin piece of fabric over the dried paint and heat-seal with an iron. Repeat with all the painted hearts.

Tips!

Tables tend to sit against a wall or out of the way of foot traffic. If your table display will be seen from both sides, consider creating the same string of hearts along both long edges of your tablecloth.

If you prefer solid hearts, add more paint as you're blotting with your sponge until it's a solid color.

If you prefer a smaller or larger tablecloth, shorten or lengthen the 87-inch fabric dimension to suit.

This tablecloth is machine washable, but line-drying is recommended.

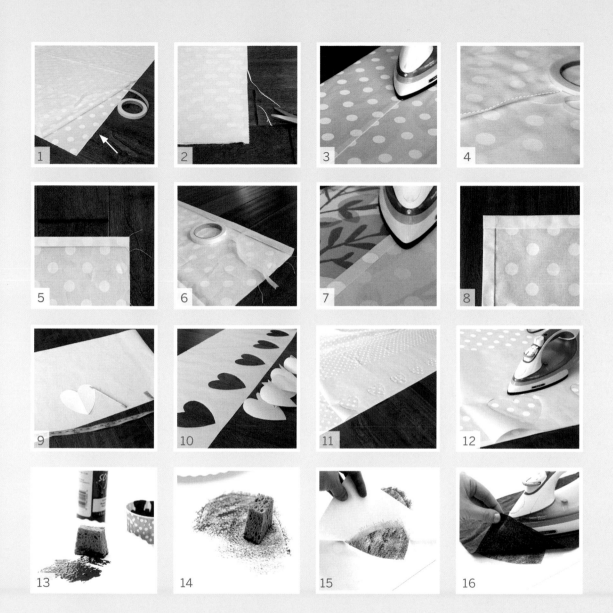

FABRIC SCRAP EASTER EGGS

Create the perfect addition to your spring décor by adding these little eggs to a basket or bowl on your table, placing them on a mantel, or hiding them in and around your other spring décor. They're also a great way to use up all those little scraps of fabric (I know you have a pile) that you can't seem to get rid of!

SKILL LEVEL: I » TIME ESTIMATE: 60 MINUTES

Supplies

- Cotton fabric scraps, separated by color
- Fabric decoupage sealer
- Sponge brush
- 4-inch smooth Styrofoam eggs (I used 6)
- Wax paper
- Spray gloss sealer

Toolkit

- Scissors

1. Cut your fabric scraps into strips, varying from ½ to 1 inch wide and anywhere from 2 to 4 inches long. Really, most dimensions work, so don't bother measuring. Just eyeball it and start cutting. Sort the strips into piles by color.

2. Apply just a bit of decoupage sealer to the back (wrong) side of one of the strips of fabric with your sponge brush.

3. Press this strip, sealer facing down, onto an egg and smooth it out with your fingers. Then paint another layer of decoupage sealer on the front side of the fabric, overlapping onto the egg, and smooth out any bubbles or excess sealer with your sponge brush.

4. Continue to add strips of fabric, making sure that there is a layer of decoupage sealer on both sides of the strips. Add a variety of colors of strips to the egg, or keep each egg one color tone. After a while, there will be enough decoupage sealer on the egg that you don't need to add a layer to the back side of each fabric strip. Just lay the fabric on top of the sealer that's already on the egg.

5. Continue adding strips until the egg is completely covered.

6. Repeat with your other eggs and fabric strips. Allow the eggs to dry completely on a piece of wax paper and then spray each egg on all sides with a spray gloss sealer.

Tips!

There are two different types of three-dimensional foam shapes that I've seen available for purchase. One type of Styrofoam is pretty rough and porous. The other is a smooth and paintable foam and works best for this project.

If all you have is regular decoupage sealer (not the fabric variety), go ahead and use it. I've used it for fabric projects, and it also works well.

FABRIC GIFT BOW

Making your own gift bows is truly a great way to add a little love to your gifts, any time of year. And even better is that these little guys will help you use up your ever-growing scrap pile.

SKILL LEVEL: I » TIME ESTIMATE: 30 MINUTES

Supplies

- Cotton fabric scraps or burlap
- Hot glue gun and glue sticks

Toolkit

- Scissors
- Pinking shears
- Ruler

1. Use your pinking shears to cut ten strips of fabric 1 inch wide. Three strips should be 11 inches long, three strips should be 10 inches long, three strips should be 9 inches long, and one strip should be 4½ inches long.

2. Lay one of the longest strips of fabric right side down in front of you. Take one end and loop it around back onto itself and hot glue it facedown onto about the middle of the wrong side of this strip of fabric.

3. Loop the other end onto itself in the same way and glue it down with a small dot of hot glue, creating a symmetrical figure-eight shape. The ends will overlap about 1 inch. (It may help to first create your figure-eight shape without gluing, compare it to the photo, and get a feel for where to glue and overlap.)

4. Repeat with the other eight longer strips of fabric. Save the shortest strip of fabric for later.

5. Grab two of the longest figure-eights and cross them, creating an X shape (not a plus shape). Glue them together with a small dab of glue.

6. Glue the third longest figure-eight shape on top, creating a symmetrical bow base, with six equally spaced points.

7. Next take one of the 10-inch figure-eights and glue it on top, placing the points evenly between the points of the base below.

8. Add the other two 10-inch figure-eights and glue them down, keeping the spacing the same as the base layer but placing each of the points in between two of the points from the base layer below.

9. Glue in place the next size of figure-eights to create a third layer of points, spacing them between the points of the second layer.

10. Loop your 4½-inch-long strip of fabric into a circle, overlapping the ends by 1 inch and gluing them in place.

11. Glue the loop in the center of the bow.

Tips!

If you decide to make burlap bows, use the same strip dimensions as above, but instead of using pinking shears to cut the strips (they won't have the same effect on burlap), measure out your 1-inch width and then tug on one of the woven strings of the burlap that runs parallel to where you would need to cut it.

Pull the string all the way out, leaving a wider and straight area to cut your strips from. Trust me, this will save you some burlap headaches!

Will these bows fray? Very, very minimally. And hey, if they do, it just gives them a cute shabby look.

If you'd like to make a smaller bow (like the blue one pictured on page 178), cut the strips ¾ inch wide and cut three strips of each of the following lengths: 9, 8, and 7 inches. Cut the smallest strip for the center loop at 2½ inches. Construct them in the same way as the larger ones above.

When using the hot glue, only use small dots between each layer. Otherwise, your center will become too thick and heavy with all those layers of dried glue.

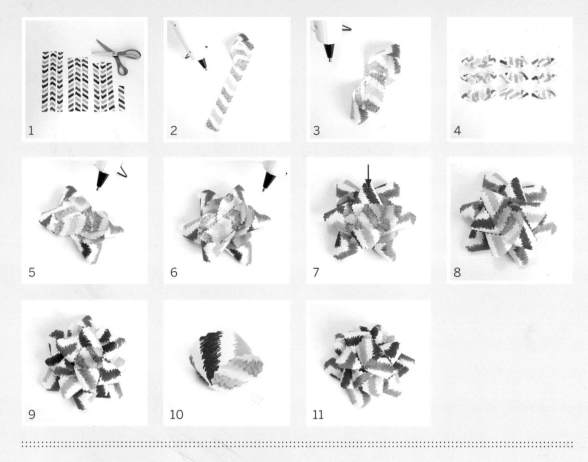

1

2

3

4

5

6

7

8

9

10

11

Tips-1

Tips-2

HALLOWEEN TABLE RUNNER

Keep Halloween fun and quirky by creating a simple table runner with dangling spiders hanging from small strands of "web" at each end. The spiders add to the charm and can be removed when the runner is cleaned and then reattached when needed. Perfect.

SKILL LEVEL: II » TIME ESTIMATE: 60 MINUTES

Supplies

- 3 yards cotton fabric (Halloween print optional)
- Double-sided fusible adhesive tape, ½ inch wide
- 6 (¼-inch) metal eyelet sets
- Eyelet setter hammer tool (or other eyelet tool)
- 6 black plastic spiders (spider rings work well)
- White quilting thread
- Epoxy glue

Toolkit

- Scissors
- Measuring tape
- Straight pins
- Iron/ironing board
- Hammer
- Pen or fine-tip marker
- Black permanent marker

The finished table runner measures 14 x 102 inches. If you prefer a shorter or longer runner, adjust accordingly.

1. Cut two pieces of fabric that measure 15 x 103 inches. Place the pieces with right sides together. Match up the sides and ends and pin in place. Unpin the fabric at one of the 15-inch-long ends and fold the top layer of fabric back a few inches. Place fusible adhesive tape along the very edge of the bottom piece (at one end) and a few inches up each side. Fold the top fabric back over, match up the edges again, and iron in place, fusing the layers together according to the adhesive's package instructions. Avoid pulling or dragging the iron across the fabric.

2. Continue down the length of the table runner, fusing the two layers together along the raw edges, about 15 or so inches at a time.

3. Once you reach the end, place fusible adhesive tape around the remaining top and bottom edges and along the end, leaving a 10-inch gap without any adhesive between the two corners (which will be used for turning it right side out). Fuse the

remaining edges together with your iron, making sure that your gap was left unfused.

4. Trim off all four corners, being careful not to cut through the adhesive completely. You are just taking away some bulk before turning it right side out so that your corners will lie flat, but you don't want to have holes when you turn your corners right side out.

5. Turn the table runner right side out through the opening, poking each corner out gently with the closed tip of your scissors. (Don't poke too hard or you'll create a hole.)

6. Fold the edges of the opening toward the inside ½ inch and iron flat. Iron the rest of the table runner flat as well.

7. Place a strip of fusible adhesive tape along the inside edge of the opening, between the layers of fabric, to close the opening. Be sure the tape won't show from the outside. Iron to seal completely shut.

8. For each eyelet that you attach to your table runner, you will need an eyelet front

(taller barrel, *a*), an eyelet back (shorter barrel, *b*), a hammer plate (*c*), and a hammer post (*d*).

9. Lay a measuring tape along one of the 14-inch-wide ends, to mark the placement of each eyelet. Place one at the 2-inch mark, the next at the 7-inch mark, and the last at

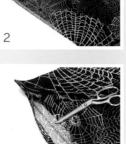

1

2

3

4

5

6

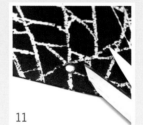

7

8

a b c d

9

10

11

12

13

14

15

16

17

18

19

20

the 12-inch mark. Place all of them about ½ inch from the bottom edge.

10. Place an eyelet back at each location and use it as a template to trace around the inside edge of the barrel.

11. Cut out the circles with scissors.

12. Place an eyelet front through one of the holes from the right side of the table runner, forcing the barrel to poke up through to the back side of the runner.

13. Flip the table runner over to the back side and fit an eyelet back around the barrel of the eyelet front piece.

14. Slide the hammer plate underneath the eyelet front and then fit the hammer post on top of the eyelet back. Tap the top of the hammer post with a regular hammer a few times, until both eyelet pieces compress and pinch the fabric in between nice and tight. Repeat with the other two holes on this end of the table runner. Repeat steps 9 through 14 at the other end of the table runner.

15. If your spiders are part of a plastic ring, cut the ring portion off.

16. Tie some quilting thread around the middle of one of the spiders, knotting it several times on the belly side of the spider. Leave the thread hanging by 12–14 inches.

17. Trim the shorter end of the thread to about ⅛ inch and then use a black permanent marker to color the thread around the spider black so that the only white thread you can see looks like it's a spider web coming out of the spider.

18. Add a dot of epoxy glue on the belly of the spider, securing the thread, and knot in place.

19. Tie the other end of the thread to the table runner through one of the eyelets.

20. Rotate the knot to the back side of the table runner, trimming down the shorter end of the thread. Attach the other five spiders to the table runner the same way, staggering the lengths of each spider if desired.

Tips!

If you can't find any Halloween-themed fabric in your local store, be sure to look online—there's so much more to choose from!

APPLIQUÉD NATIVITY ON BURLAP

Sometimes simple is best, especially when it comes to making a holiday decoration. And you know, there's something beautiful about mixing the raw texture of burlap with a simple nativity silhouette. It makes me smile.

SKILL LEVEL: I » TIME ESTIMATE: 30 MINUTES

Supplies

- Nativity template (page 241)
- Printer
- Double-sided fusible adhesive (in sheets or on a roll, with paper on one side)
- Black cotton woven fabric
- Burlap cut 2 inches longer on all sides than the frame opening
- Picture frame (size is up to you)
- Scrap piece of cardboard
- Hot glue gun and glue sticks

Toolkit

- Scissors
- Ruler
- Iron/ironing board
- Scotch or masking tape
- Pencil

1. Determine what nativity template enlargement or reduction will work best for your frame size. Print the nativity on standard printer paper and tape your image to a window during daylight. (The template will be a mirror image once applied to the fabric, so take that into account at this step.)

2. Cut a piece of fusible adhesive that is slightly larger than the printed image and tape it over the image that's taped to your window. Be sure that the shiny adhesive side is facing the window and the paper side is facing you.

3. Trace around the image with a pencil, drawing on the paper side of the fusible adhesive.

4. Cut a piece of your black fabric that is slightly larger than your fusible adhesive piece. Place the fusible adhesive onto the wrong side of your black fabric, with your drawn image facing up. Follow the instructions of your particular fusible adhesive and fuse your image onto the fabric. (Don't overheat or the adhesive will burn and will be useless.)

5. Cut around each of the figures in the image, cutting through the fusible adhesive and fabric together.

6. Peel the paper backing of the adhesive off the fabric.

7. Arrange your manger scene onto the burlap, with the adhesive side facing down. Hold your frame over the top to check your placement, adjust, and check again. Iron the manger scene in place according to the adhesive's package instructions.

8. Cut a piece of cardboard that is the same size as your frame opening. Center the cardboard onto the back side of your burlap and then fold each of the edges around the back of the cardboard, securing with hot glue.

9. Place the cardboard and burlap into the frame and secure the back.

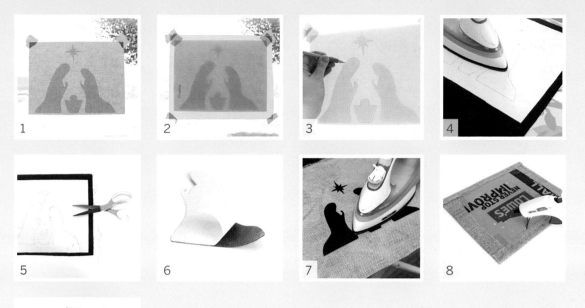

Tips!

Whether you keep the glass in the frame depends on your preference. I like the look without the glass because there's no glare, and it looks more custom and raw.

CHRISTMAS TREE SKIRT

Don't let your tree sit there bare naked! Cover up her unmentionables (the tree stand) with a simple tree skirt adorned with large snowflakes. Once you add it to your holiday décor, you'll use it year after year!

SKILL LEVEL: II » TIME ESTIMATE: 90 MINUTES

Supplies

- 1½ yards red felt (polyester or wool), 51-plus inches wide
- Cotton string
- 4½ inches Velcro, ½ inch wide
- Epoxy glue
- Snowflake templates (pages 242–249)
- ½ yard white felt (polyester or wool), 51-plus inches wide

Toolkit

- Scissors
- Measuring tape
- Permanent marker
- Straight pins

Photos for steps 1 through 7 show a mini version of the actual size, to help demonstrate the process a little easier.

1. Cut out a 51 x 51-inch square of red felt. If your felt has a wrong side, place it wrong side up.

2. Tie one end of a piece of string to a straight pin and the other end near the tip of a permanent marker. The string should measure exactly 25 inches between the two when pulled taut.

3. Mark the exact middle of the square piece of felt. Stick the pin on that mark and hold it there firmly with one hand while you pull the string and marker straight out with your other hand, making sure there's no slack in the string. Rotate the marker around the center point, making a curved line on the fabric as you rotate it around the pin.

4. Continue all the way around until you complete the circle, which should be 50 inches in diameter.

Tips!

When using epoxy glue, it helps to apply pressure as it's drying. Place something heavy, like a book, on top of the felt and Velcro pieces while the glue dries completely.

5. Draw another smaller circle (5 inches in diameter) at the exact center of the larger circle. You can shorten the string to 2½ inches and trace it as you did for the larger one.

6. Use a ruler to draw a straight line from the smaller circle to the larger one.

7. Cut out the larger circle and set aside the outer felt scraps. Then cut up the straight line and cut out the smaller circle as well.

8. Cut three rectangles from your red felt scraps, 3½ x 1¾ inches each. Cut three pieces of the soft side of your Velcro, 1½ x 1½ inches each. Repeat with the scratchy side of your Velcro.

9. Using epoxy glue, secure a soft Velcro piece (fuzzy side up) to one end of a felt rectangle piece. Repeat with the other two felt and two soft Velcro pieces.

10. Turn each of the rectangle pieces facedown and place the non-Velcro end onto the straight edge of the circle opening, overlapping by about 1½ inches. Space them evenly along this straight edge and glue in place.

11. Glue the corresponding scratchy Velcro pieces to the other straight edge of the circle opening.

12. Fasten the flaps to be sure that the Velcro is positioned just right, so the circle closes completely. Make any adjustments you need before the glue dries. Then apply pressure as the glue sets.

13. Cut out the paper snowflake templates and trace them onto the white felt with a permanent marker. Cut out three snowflakes from each of the three templates, making nine total snowflakes. (As you cut, remove the marker lines as much as you can.)

14. Arrange all nine snowflakes evenly around the tree skirt, about 1½ inches from the outer edge. Pick up one snowflake at a time and add glue to the underside. Press firmly back onto the tree skirt and apply pressure as it dries.

Chapter 6

RE-PURPOSING

SWEATER INTO COASTERS

Wait! Don't get rid of that old wool sweater! Felt it and then turn it into cozy and simple little coasters. A sweater in its normal woven state has a variety of strands, from very loose to very tightly woven, depending on the sweater style. If you cut it, the fibers will unravel. "Felting" a wool sweater will tighten up the fibers so that when cut, the sweater won't unravel. Then you can use it for whatever you want, without worrying about the edges coming undone. Your mug (and wallet) will thank you!

SKILL LEVEL: I » TIME ESTIMATE: 20 MINUTES (not including the felting process)

Supplies

- 100-percent wool sweater
- 4-inch circular cork coaster bases
- Hot glue gun and glue sticks

Toolkit

- Scissors
- Washer/dryer

1. To "felt" your sweater, throw the sweater into the washing machine and turn the setting to hot. Make sure your machine is set for free motion (not a delicate cycle), because the more agitation the better. In fact, if you have other things to wash, throw those in there to give the wool extra items to rub against, speeding up the felting process.

2. Dry the sweater on high heat, which will tighten the fibers up even more. Once you've removed it from the dryer, you should see a noticeable difference in the size of your sweater, and the fibers should look more dense and fuzzy, like felt fabric. If not, repeat the washing and drying as many times as it takes to felt it.

3. If you're unsure whether your sweater has properly felted, cut into it and test it. You should be able to pull at the cut edges and not have any unraveling occur. If it does, repeat the washing and drying again. (And consider yourself lucky that you're getting extra laundry done along with it!)

4. Once your sweater has properly felted, use a coaster as a guide to cut a circle out of your sweater. Don't worry about getting it perfect because you will trim the sweater down more later on.

5. Place a generous amount of hot glue onto a small section of one side of a cork coaster, being careful to keep the glue from oozing over the edge.

6. Center the felted sweater circle on top of the coaster, pressing it down firmly where the glue has already been placed. Lift up the sweater and continue to add small sections of glue, press firmly, and repeat.

7. Trim off any excess sweater, nice and even with the edges of the coaster.

8. Repeat for as many coasters you'd like and have felt for.

Tips!

Having a top-load washer versus a front loader may affect the number of times you have to wash the sweater to get it to felt (a top-loader felts a little faster), but I have felted sweaters in both types of machines, so don't let that deter you!

My favorite place to find wool sweaters to felt is the thrift store. You can find some serious treasures there!

PLACEMAT INTO THROW PILLOW

One of the fastest and least expensive ways to change your home décor is to change your throw pillows. And to continue with the whole "simple" (and inexpensive) thing, how about grabbing one of your old placemats (especially if you have a set that you no longer use because a few of them are stained) and turning it into a fun new throw pillow? Or go out and buy a few new placemats in the exact colors you want—I won't tell!

SKILL LEVEL: 1 » TIME ESTIMATE: 20 MINUTES

Supplies

- 1 fabric placemat (12 x 18 inches or larger and safe to iron)
- Double-sided fusible adhesive tape, ½ inch wide
- Polyester fiberfill

Toolkit

- Scissors
- Measuring tape
- Iron/ironing board

1. Iron your placemat flat, releasing any wrinkles.

2. Fold your placemat in half widthwise, wrong sides together. Iron this fold flat.

3. Open up the placemat and place a strip of fusible adhesive tape along the fold, making sure it reaches all the way from one side of the placemat to the other.

4. Fold the placemat in half again (along the original fold) and iron to fuse the adhesive in place according to the adhesive's package instructions. Avoid pulling or dragging the iron across the fabric.

5. Open the placemat up again and place fusible adhesive tape along the sides of the lower portion of the placemat (on the wrong side of the placemat). Also place fusible adhesive tape along the bottom edge, but leave about a 5-inch gap at the

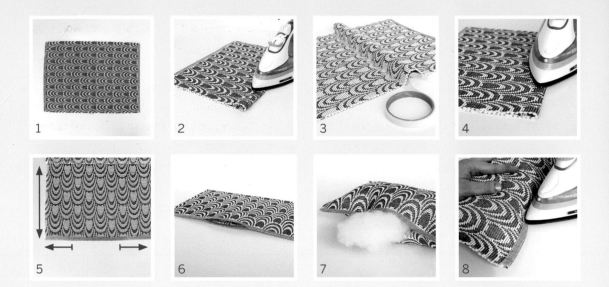

center of the bottom edge for stuffing the pillow. (Use the arrows on photo 5 as a guide for placement.)

6. Fold the placemat closed again, line up all the edges, and be sure that the adhesive is lined up with the edges as well and not peeking out. Iron to fuse the layers together.

7. Open up the 5-inch gap and stuff it with fiberfill. You'll need enough to plump up the pillow but not too much or you won't be able to close the pillow.

8. Push all of the stuffing away from the opening the best you can and then place a 5-inch-long strip of fusible adhesive tape along the inside edge of the opening. Pinch the two layers closed, make sure the adhesive is completely hidden, and iron to fuse the opening closed.

Tips!

Be sure to check the placemat material and verify that it can be ironed.

Fold your placemat in half and check to see if all edges and corners match up pretty well before beginning. If not, your pillow will be uneven.

SHIRT INTO GIRL'S SKIRT

Do you have trouble finding cute knit fabric by the yard? Cut up an old knit T-shirt instead (in any color or print you can get your hands on) and turn it into a darling little skirt for girls. Don't you just love turning old into new?

SKILL LEVEL: I   »   TIME ESTIMATE: 20 MINUTES

Supplies

- 1 old knit T-shirt (extra-large size offers more material to work with)
- Double-sided fusible adhesive tape, ½ inch wide
- Elastic, 1 inch wide (amount depends on waist measurement)

Toolkit

- Scissors
- Straight pins
- Ruler or hem guide ruler
- Iron/ironing board
- Safety pin

Measure your subject's waist and have a desired skirt length in mind.

1. To find a shirt that will work well for this skirt project, make sure that the measurement of usable fabric (generally below the sleeves and down to the bottom of the shirt) is at least the length that you'd like your skirt to be, plus 2 inches, and that the circumference is at least 1½ to 2 times the waist measurement. This will give the skirt a sufficient gather.

2. Cut off the top portion of the shirt, leaving the remaining piece 2 inches longer than the desired skirt length. (Cut length only off the top because you will be using the hem of the shirt as the new hem of the skirt.)

3. Turn the fabric tube inside out and fold the upper cut edge over ¾ inch, wrong sides together. Iron in place.

4. Fold the upper edge over again by 1¼ inches. Iron your fold flat.

5. Lift up the fold and start lining your fusible adhesive tape right along the folded edge.

6. Continue placing fusible adhesive tape all the way around the upper fold, leaving a 3-inch gap in the back where you'll insert your elastic. Fold the fabric back down on the original fold. Pin your fold in place all the way around.

7. Iron the adhesive in place according to the adhesive's package instructions, making sure that the adhesive is properly fused and that there's an opening along the back. (Avoid pulling or dragging the iron across the fabric.) This will serve as the casing for your elastic.

8. Cut a piece of elastic that is the waist measurement, plus 1 inch. Attach a safety pin to one end of your elastic and insert it into the opening of the casing.

9. Push the safety pin along inside the casing, pulling the elastic with it as you go, making sure that the other end of elastic remains on the outside of the skirt.

10. Once you reach the end, make sure your elastic isn't twisted and that both ends are coming out of the casing.

11. Remove the safety pin and overlap the two ends by 2 inches.

12. Place two strips of fusible adhesive tape between the elastic where they overlap. For an even better hold, double up on the adhesive and place two layers of it between the elastic.

13. Iron the overlapped elastic in place to fuse the layers.

14. Adjust the waistband and elastic until the elastic is completely enclosed within the casing. Find the opening of the casing, pull the fabric flat, and place a piece of fusible adhesive tape along the bottom fold of the opening.

15. Iron the opening closed, making sure that the fabric of the casing is laying flat and isn't bunched up at all from the elastic.

16. Distribute the fabric evenly around the elastic and then lightly iron the gathers of the waistband to help the fabric lie a little flatter.

Tips!

Knit shirts all hang and feel a little different. While deciding which shirt to cut up, hold it up and notice how it drapes. Decide if it would hang well as a skirt or not. (Ladies' shirts tend to work better for projects such as these. Try looking for something other than a stiff old T-shirt you'd mow the lawn in; something a little softer and with more give works better.)

The larger the shirt, the more you have to gather it, yielding a fuller skirt. However, you don't want to gather in so much that you're forcing a lot of fabric on the elastic, resulting in a bulky waistband.

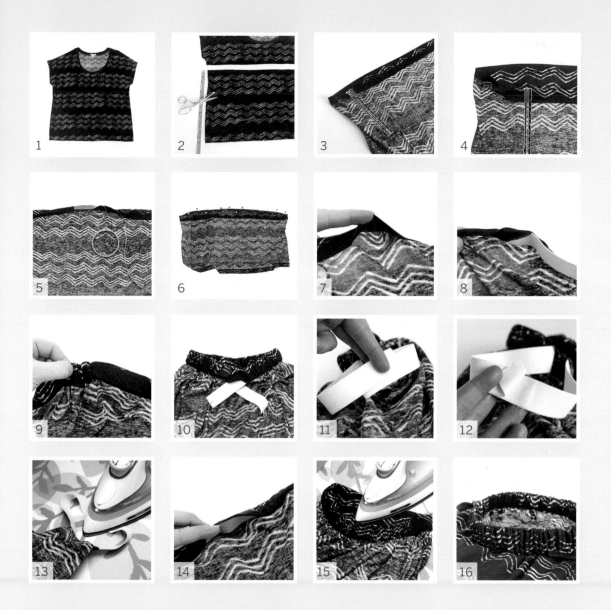

CLOTH NAPKIN INTO KID'S HALF APRON

Kids are messy little creatures. Instead of fretting about them leaning over the mixing bowl and dirtying up their clothes or getting messy while helping out with chores, turn an old cloth napkin into the fastest little apron you'll ever make. But even more important than keeping them clean is how special you'll make them feel with their "work" apron on, ready to help with whatever task you've given them.

SKILL LEVEL: I » TIME ESTIMATE: 30 MINUTES

Supplies

- Cloth napkin (18-inch square or larger)
- Double-sided fusible adhesive tape, ½ inch wide
- Grosgrain ribbon, 1½ inches wide (amount depends on size)

Toolkit

- Scissors
- Ruler or hem guide ruler
- Iron/ironing board
- Safety pin
- Lighter

1. Start with an old or mismatched cloth napkin or buy a new funky print to transform into an apron.

2. Open up the napkin and place it right side down in front of you. Fold down the top edge 2½ inches. Iron flat.

3. Open up the top flap and place some of your fusible adhesive tape on the upper edge of the folded piece (that you just opened back up). Put the flap back down and iron in place according to the adhesive's package instructions, creating a casing for the ribbon to slide through.

4. Cut a piece of ribbon that is 70 inches long (more or less, depending on the size of the child) and use a lighter to carefully melt and heat-seal the ends to keep them from fraying.

5. Attach a safety pin to one end of the ribbon and slide it through the casing that you just created at the top of the napkin.

6. Pull the ribbon all the way through, until both ribbon ends are the same length. Remove the safety pin and place the apron face up in front of you. At one end of the casing, lift up the fabric just a bit and slide a 2-inch-long piece of fusible adhesive tape between the fabric and the ribbon, lining the adhesive up with the outer edge of the fabric. Iron until the adhesive is set. Repeat on the other side.

T-SHIRT INTO
5-STRAND HEADBAND

I know you're hoarding a few old, stained T-shirts in the bottom of your dresser drawer, and you think you'll find a use for them "someday." Well, that "someday" is here! Pull them out and let them do you some good by keeping that hair out of your face!

SKILL LEVEL: I » TIME ESTIMATE: 45 MINUTES

Supplies

- Jersey knit T-shirt (solid or a variety of colors)
- Cotton string
- Epoxy glue

Toolkit

- Scissors
- Flexible measuring tape
- Masking tape

1. Grab an old T-shirt and take note of how it stretches. Usually T-shirts stretch more from side to side and not as much (if at all) from top to bottom. Each headband strip needs some stretch, so choose a few stretchy ones. First cut off the bottom hem around the shirt and then begin cutting horizontal strips from the shirt, which will still allow for some stretch.

2. Cut five strips, each about 2 inches wide; the length is variable, depending on the size of head and how much your fabric stretches. A good guide is to make the strip length twice the length of the head circumference measurement. Just cut each of the strips straight across the shirt tube and then cut open one of the side seams, making one long strip. You can trim the excess later if needed.

3. Pull the ends of each strip in opposite directions to release some of the stretch. The edges will most likely curl, but if they don't, that's okay.

4. Tie the ends of the five strips together with some string, about an inch from the ends.

5. Tape the strands onto a table above the knot. Separate your strands into two groups: three strands on the left and two on the right. (For clarity, I have used five different colors of knit to demonstrate the five-strand braid and will call each strand by its color.)

6. Grab the yellow strand all the way on the left . . .

7. . . . and cross it over the gray strand to its right.

8. Grab the blue strand . . .

9. . . . and cross it over the yellow strand to its left.

10. Pull the yellow strand from this left group and add it to the right side group.

11. You still have two groups, but now there are two strands on the left and three on the right.

12. Now do the same to the right side group, but in mirror image. Grab the pink strand all the way on the right . . .

13. . . . and cross it over the green strand to its left.

14. Grab the yellow strand . . .

15. . . . and cross it over the pink strand to its right.

16. Pull the pink strand from this right group and add it to the left side group.

17. Repeat steps 6 through 16 until your braid takes shape (Take note that as you work, the colors will move to different positions. Reference the placement of the strands, rather than the colors, in the instructions as you braid.). As you braid, be sure to keep each strand pulled snug but not so tight that it takes all the stretch out of it.

18. Once you reach the end (or as long as you need it), tie another string at the ends to secure the strands and keep them from unraveling.

19. Join the two ends of the braid and tie them together with more string. Trim off the ends.

20. To hide this tied section, cut a rectangle of fabric from the T-shirt that is wide enough to cover the tied ends of your braid and long enough to wrap around the braid about 1½ times. Slide it under the tied ends and add a line of epoxy glue to one end of your piece of fabric.

21. Fold the end up onto the braid and press firmly to adhere to the fabric.

22. Wrap the other end of the fabric piece around the loose ends and fold the end in enough to overlap the first end. Add another line of glue.

23. Press firmly and let dry completely before wearing.

Tips!

If you don't have a shirt to cut up, you can purchase knit from the fabric store. Jersey knit works great for this project. Be sure that you're cutting with the stretch so that each strip stretches if you pull from each end.

When deciding how long to make the headband, you will want the finished braid about an inch or two less than the head measurement. It will stretch a bit when worn, and you want it to fit snug around the head.

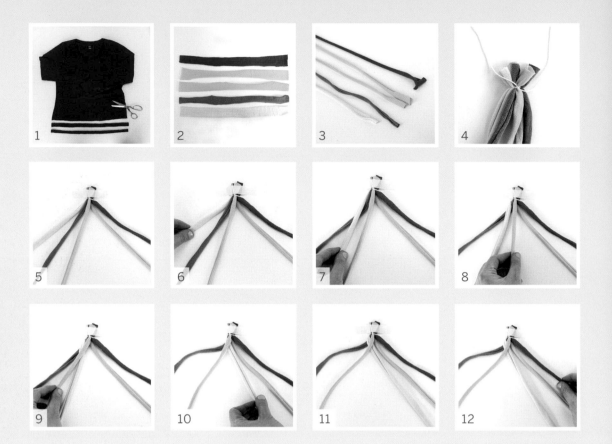

13

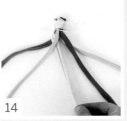

14

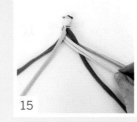

15

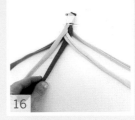

16

17

18

19

20

21

22

23

SCRAP CARDBOARD INTO TISSUE BOX COVER

We have almost year-round allergy sufferers in our home, so tissue boxes sit in every room. Instead of cringing over the newest obnoxious tissue box packaging, I created a reusable cover to slide right over the top, allowing the tissues to become part of our home décor. It's a win-win!

SKILL LEVEL: II » TIME ESTIMATE: 60 MINUTES

Supplies

- Scrap pieces of cardboard
- Square tissue box
- Hot glue gun and glue sticks
- ¼ yard felt (100 percent polyester)
- ¼ yard cotton quilting fabric (any color or print)
- Decoupage sealer, any variety
- Sponge brush

Toolkit

- Scissors
- Ruler
- Utility knife
- Cutting mat
- Pen or tailor's chalk

1. Gather pieces of cardboard that are larger than the sides of your tissue box.

2. Since you'll be doubling the cardboard layers to make it sturdier, hold up two pieces of the cardboard along one side of the tissue box and then measure the width of the tissue box including the two layers of cardboard. This is the width you need for your cardboard pieces. (The one pictured measures 4½ inches.)

3. Measure the height of the tissue box. This is the height you need for your cardboard pieces. (The one pictured measures 5 inches.)

4. Use a ruler to measure out and draw eight of these square(ish) pieces on the cardboard. (The ones pictured measure 4½ x 5 inches.)

5. Use a utility knife to carefully cut out all eight squares.

6. Apply hot glue to one side of one square.

7. Place another square on top and sandwich the two pieces together. Repeat with the other squares, making four total square pieces for the four sides of the cover.

8. Hot glue two of the squares together along their sides (make sure it's the sides you're gluing together, not the top or bottom), at a 90-degree angle, butting one end up to the other.

9. Add another line of hot glue on the inside only, to offer extra stability.

10. Continue hot gluing the rest of the sides together by having one end overlap the other, making it symmetrical all the way around. Add a line of hot glue to the inside of the other three corners where the cardboard meets.

11. Trace the opening in the tissue box cover with a pen and cut it out with your utility knife.

12. Find the exact center of this top piece, mark it with a dot, and then decide how large you'd like your tissue box opening. This can vary, depending on how large or small the original tissue box opening is and on your preference. (The opening pictured

is 2 x 3 inches.) Measure out from the center dot.

13. Cut out the opening and use that as a template to cut out an identical piece from another scrap of cardboard.

14. Add hot glue to a side of one of the top pieces and then sandwich them together.

15. Hot glue the top piece to the cube.

16. Cut out a piece of felt that is the same size as the top (including the opening) and hot glue it in place.

17. Cut a strip of felt that is the exact height of the tissue box cover and long enough to wrap all the way around. Use hot glue to attach it to the box.

18. Once you've glued all the way around, trim off any excess felt if necessary, so that the ends meet up without overlapping.

19. Cut out a square piece of your cotton quilting fabric to cover the top of the tissue box cover, with about an inch of excess on all sides. Place the fabric right side down and then place the tissue box top face down, right on top of the fabric. Center the box on the fabric and then trace the rectangle opening right onto the fabric with tailor's chalk or a pen.

20. Cut a diagonal line from one corner of the rectangle to the opposite one. Repeat with the opposite corners and be sure not to cut through the traced line.

21. Place the fabric right on top of the box, centering the "X" on top of the box opening.

22. Apply a bit of hot glue to each of the triangle flaps (on the wrong side of the fabric) and then wrap them to the inside of the box and press firmly in place.

23. Be sure that each flap was pulled smoothly into place.

24. Cut a square out of each corner of fabric, cutting right up to the corner of the box but not through it.

25. Smooth down each side, creating a nice sharp corner. Repeat with the other three corners and hot glue all the sides down.

26. Measure all the way around the sides of your felt-covered box and then measure the height. Cut a piece of fabric that is 1 inch wider and 2 inches taller than those measurements. (The fabric pictured is 23 x 7¾ inches.) Verify that the fabric strip is the right size by wrapping it all the way around the box and see if it overlaps by an inch. Then fold over one of the long sides of your piece of fabric by ½ inch. Iron in place.

27. Place the box on its side and line up its upper edge along the folded edge of fabric, starting ½ inch from the raw end of the fabric strip.

28. Fold that extra ½ inch of fabric up onto the side of the box and hot glue in place.

29. Continue adding hot glue liberally all over the wrong side of the fabric, especially along the top folded edge. (Be careful not to let it ooze above the top edge.) Add glue in small sections at a time, pressing in place after each application.

30. Be sure to match up the fold of the fabric strip with the upper edge of the box, paying close attention to the corners. You want to cover the felt and any raw fabric edges from underneath.

31. Once you have almost covered the entire box, stop about 2 inches before you reach the spot where you started gluing. You should have about ½ inch of excess fabric hanging past the first corner. If you have a little more than that from pulling your fabric as you were gluing it around, trim it down so that there's only ½ inch of excess remaining.

32. Fold that ½ inch toward the inside, matching the fold with the corner of the box.

33. Hot glue the fold in place, keeping the glue hidden and toward the inside.

34. Cut a slit at each of the bottom corners, perpendicular to the bottom edge of the box. Cut right up to the box's corner but not through it.

35. Fold each flap up into the inside of the box and hot glue in place.

36. Repeat with the other three flaps, keeping the fabric pulled taut.

37. Cut four rectangles of felt that fit on the inner sides of the box. Hot glue them in place.

38. Cut another square of felt with a rectangle opening that fits on the underside of the top of the box. Hot glue in place.

39. To prevent the fabric on the inner corners of the box opening from fraying, add little dabs of decoupage sealer with a sponge brush to any raw edges that you see. (These cuts were made on the diagonal so fraying should be minimal, but adding a bit of decoupage sealer will help keep them stiff.)

Tips!

Sometimes the width measurement on one side of a square tissue box is wider than the other sides. Use the widest width for your measurements and then you'll be sure the cover fits.

If you prefer to make a rectangular tissue box cover, you'll need to adjust the measurements and make long sections for the two longer sides, but the process is still the same.

If you are using really thick and sturdy pieces of cardboard, you won't need to double the layers. If that's the case, just use a single layer of cardboard.

The purpose of lining the inside of the box with felt is to cover the raw ends of fabric, but it also creates a snug fit over the actual tissue box.

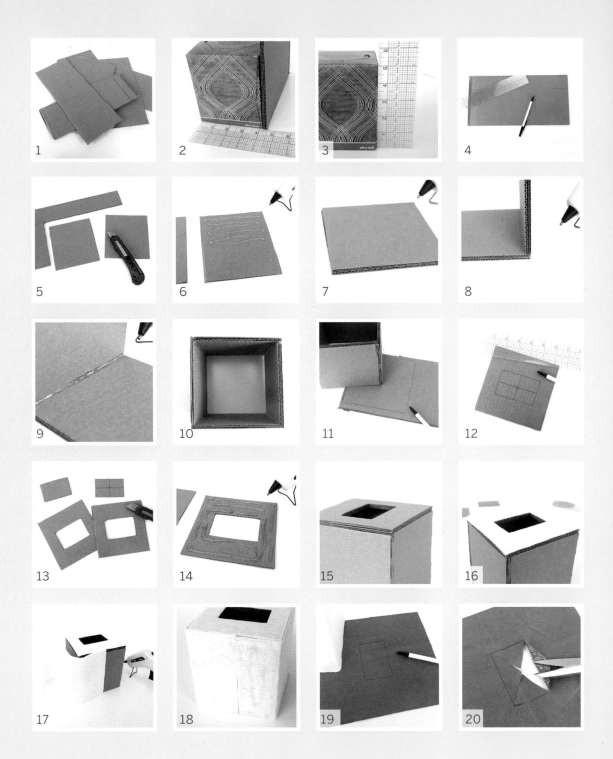

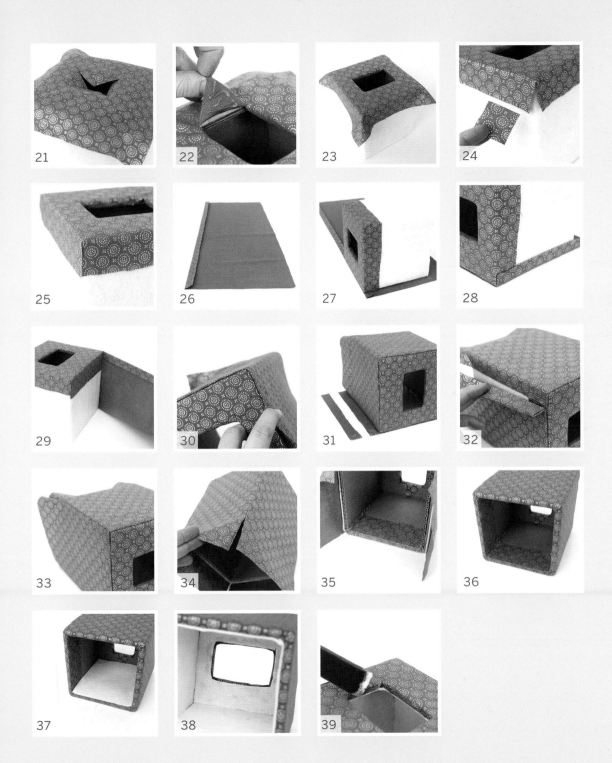

SWEATER INTO FRUIT COZY

Have you ever thrown an apple or pear into your bag for a midday snack? If so, you know that the odds of your fruit coming out unscathed are slim. Avoid bruised fruit by creating a "felted" sweater cuff to slide around your fruit, and then marvel at the usefulness in that sweater's second life.

SKILL LEVEL: I » TIME ESTIMATE: 10 MINUTES (not including the felting process)

Supplies

- 100-percent wool sweater (one with a wide-ribbed cuff)

Toolkit

- Scissors
- Washer/dryer

1. To "felt" your sweater, throw the sweater into the washing machine and turn the setting to hot. Make sure your machine is set for free motion (not a delicate cycle), because the more agitation the better. In fact, if you have other things to wash, throw those in there to give the wool extra items to rub against, speeding up the felting process.

2. Dry the sweater on high heat, which will tighten the fibers up even more. Once you've removed it from the dryer, you should see a noticeable difference in the size of your sweater, and the fibers should look more dense and fuzzy, like felt fabric. If not, repeat the washing and drying as many times as it takes to felt it.

3. If you're unsure whether your sweater has properly felted, cut into the sweater and test it. You should be able to pull at the cut edges and not have any unraveling occur. If it does, repeat the washing and drying again.

4. Now you're ready to create your fruit cozy. Cut the ribbed cuff off, right where the weaving of the fibers changes and becomes less bulky on the sleeve. See? Isn't that great? No unraveling!

Tips!

Having a top-load washer versus a front loader may affect the number of times you have to wash the sweater to get it to felt (a top loader felts a little faster), but I have felted sweaters in both types of machines, so don't let that deter you!

My favorite place to find wool sweaters to felt is the thrift store. You can find some serious treasures there!

You don't have to have a ribbed cuff to use as the cozy. You could felt a sweater and use a section of the sleeve that has felted down small enough to use around your fruit. The ribbing does, however, add a little more padding.

PLASTIC BOTTLE INTO WATER BOTTLE SLING

How many times have you thrown away an old plastic bottle or container and wondered if you could've gotten any other use out of it? Well, save some space in your recycling bin (and free up your hands) by turning them into water bottle slings. This is useful for all ages but is especially helpful for kiddos who want to keep track of their own water bottle on long walks or hikes.

SKILL LEVEL: I   »   TIME ESTIMATE: 30 MINUTES

Supplies

- Empty cylindrical plastic container (large enough to fit a water bottle)
- Grosgrain ribbon (amount depends on size)
- Epoxy glue

Toolkit

- Heavy-duty scissors
- Ruler
- Permanent marker
- Lighter
- Clothespins or a heavy book

1. Peel away any wrappers or labels from the container.

2. Decide how tall you'd like your holder to be. (The one pictured is 5 inches tall.) Use a permanent marker and a ruler to draw a straight line where you'll make your cut.

3. Cut slightly below the line so that the marker line will be cut off.

4. If you're having a hard time cutting the curved container, trim it down in smaller pieces.

5. Draw a very narrow rectangle shape on one side of your container (about 1 inch below the top), where your ribbon will slide through. Be sure that it's slightly wider than the ribbon width.

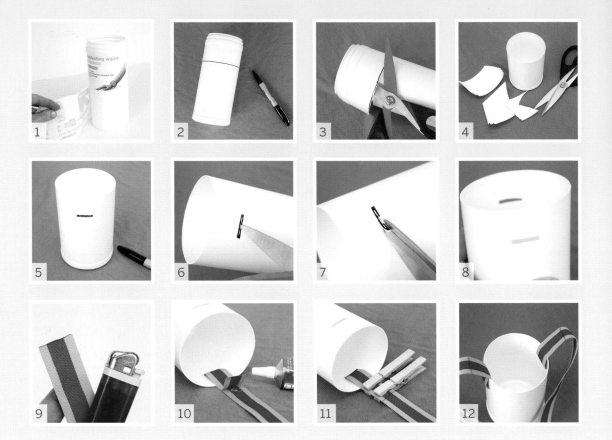

6. To cut the rectangle-shaped slit, poke the tip of your scissors through first.

7. Cut around the outside edge of the marker lines, to remove them completely from the container.

8. Make an identical narrow slit on the opposite side of the container, the same distance down from the top.

9. Measure your subject (up and across the chest and then back down) to see how long the strap needs to be and then add 3 inches to that measurement. Cut the ribbon to that length. Carefully melt the cut ends of the ribbon with a lighter to heat-seal them to keep them from fraying.

10. Slide one end of the ribbon through the container from the outside. Pull the end of the ribbon from the inside and overlap it back on itself 1½ inches. Lay the container down on its side and add some epoxy glue between where the ribbon overlaps.

11. Press down firmly and use clothespins or a heavy book to help keep the ribbon pieces pressed firmly together while the glue dries.

12. Repeat with the other end of ribbon, first making sure that the ribbon isn't twisted.

Tips!

If your container has images or type printed right onto it, consider spray painting it before adding your ribbon.

If you feel more comfortable using a utility knife instead of scissors to cut the container, go ahead. I tend to have more control and make more precise cuts with scissors, but use what's best for you.

T-SHIRT INTO FRINGE SKIRT

Dig through your clothing-donation pile and give some old knit T-shirts a second life by turning them into a flouncy fringe skirt. The skirt will bounce and twirl as your little girl moves, giving her outfit a unique twist. And just think—it didn't cost you a thing!

SKILL LEVEL: I » **TIME ESTIMATE: 60 MINUTES**

Supplies

- Old knit T-shirts
- Cord elastic (amount depends on waist measurement)

Toolkit

- Scissors
- Flexible measuring tape

1. Decide on the skirt length you need. Double that number and add 1 inch.

2. Cut off the bottom hem and the side seams of the shirts you're using.

3. Cut sections out of the shirt (vertically) that are the correct length measurement from step 1.

4. Cut each of these sections into strips of varying widths, between 1 and 2 inches, each strip the length of your measurement from step 1.

5. If the sleeves are long enough, use those as well.

6. Continue cutting up a variety of different shirt colors, if desired.

7. Gather enough strips for your skirt. The number needed could vary from 25 to 50 or so but will depend on your strip width and the size of skirt you're making.

8. Measure the waist of your subject and add 1 inch. Cut a piece of cord elastic the length you need for the waist. Tie the ends of your elastic together, leaving 1 inch free at each end. Slide the elastic over the curved back of a chair so that there's a gap for you to slide your strips through.

9. Grab a strip and fold it in half.

10. Drape the ends over the back of the chair and bring the loop end behind and under the elastic.

11. Pull the two ends around the elastic and down through the loop.

12. Pull the ends through gently, until a knot forms around the elastic.

13. Continue with each strip of fabric, alternating color choices. Be sure to tighten each knot the same way so they all look uniform.

14. To hide the elastic ends, tie a strip directly over one of the elastic ends . . .

15. . . . and then tie another strip over the other elastic end. This will help the elastic lie flat and stay hidden.

16. Continue all the way around the elastic, adjusting the elastic on the chair as needed. If your elastic is pulled pretty taut, you won't want to actually fill every inch of it with fabric strips. So remove it from the chair and evaluate. You still want your elastic to pull back in and have some stretch to it for a comfortable fit on your subject.

Tips!

You will be cutting vertical strips from the shirt because there is generally less stretch when you pull a shirt from the top and bottom than when you pull it from the left and right. And less stretch means the strips on your skirt will stretch a little less after it's constructed.

If you're making this for an older child and can't find T-shirts long enough for the measurements you need, consider buying jersey knit fabric. Then find the stretch of the fabric (if there's a difference vertically and horizontally) and cut against the stretch so that each strip will be less stretchy from one end to the other.

If you add too many strips of fabric, it will stretch the elastic too much and won't stay on your subject's waist.

RAMEKIN INTO PIN CUSHION

Straight pins come in handy for so many reasons: sewing, craft projects, and office use, just to name a few. Give them their own little home, made from a ramekin, teacup, or candleholder. I promise: you'll love having them corralled and ready for use.

SKILL LEVEL: II » TIME ESTIMATE: 30 MINUTES

Supplies

- Ramekin, candleholder, teacup or small mug, mini bowl, or other similarly small and hollow object
- Cotton fabric
- Hot glue gun and glue sticks
- Polyester fiberfill

Toolkit

- Scissors
- Flexible measuring tape

1. Place a flexible measuring tape over the top of your pin cushion base, creating a dome that's the same size as you'd like your cushion to be. (A good rise is about 1 inch higher than the edge.) Take note of the measurement of the dome, from one side of the base to the other.

2. Add 2 inches to this number and cut a square out of your fabric, using that width dimension. (For example, if your desired dome measurement is 5 inches across, add 2 inches and then cut a square that is 7 x 7 inches.)

3. Round off each of your corners, creating a circular shape. (It doesn't have to be perfect.)

4. Add a short line of hot glue along the inner edge of your cushion base, near the top edge.

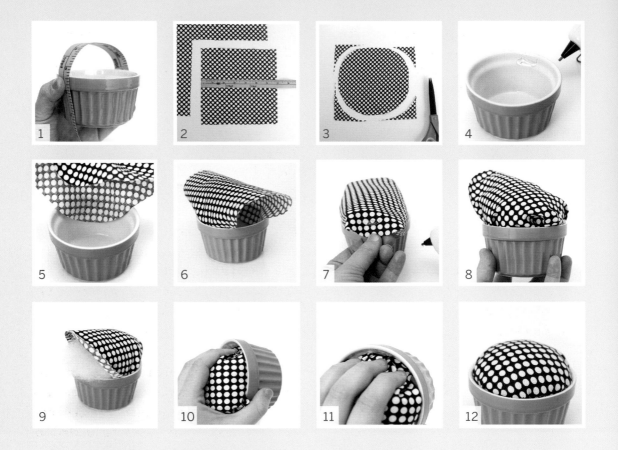

5. Place one edge of your circle onto this glue, allowing 1 inch of the fabric to drop below the rim of the base. Be sure that the right side of the fabric is facing up.

6. Glue the opposite edge of your fabric circle to the opposite inside edge of your base, allowing the edge to drop 1 inch below the rim.

7. Grab one of the sections of fabric that's still outside of the base and add some glue to the fabric, about halfway between the sections that are already glued down. Make a line of glue that's about ¾ inch from the circle's edge.

8. Tuck this fabric inside of the top edge of the base, pressing it firmly against the inside of the base. Don't worry about the edges looking smooth and perfectly tucked in yet.

9. Stuff polyester fiberfill into the dome of fabric, through the remaining side that hasn't been glued shut yet. Stuff it with enough fiberfill to help it start to take shape.

10. Begin evening out the sides that you've already glued, adding more glue to the gaps. Try to create a smooth domed look, gluing down the fabric evenly all the way around. Stuffing more fiberfill in a little at a time can help push out the fabric more, showing you where you may need to glue your fabric a little better. It also helps to use your fingers to pull away the fabric a bit from the base, making more room to add glue to the inside edge of the base.

11. Stuff more fiberfill under the fabric until your dome is nice and firm and your fabric is taut. Use your fingers to tuck the remaining fabric inside of the base and then add a line of glue to the inner edge of the base. Press the fabric against the glue.

12. Add glue where needed around the base, to create an even and rounded dome shape.

Headboard drawing guides (for Tufted Headboard, page 47)

KING-SIZE HEADBOARD

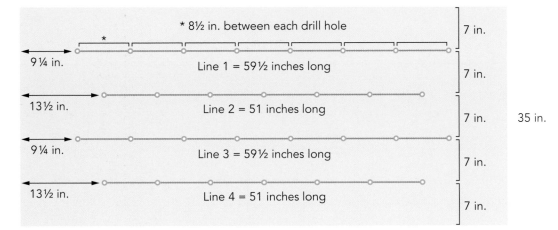

* 8½ in. between each drill hole — 7 in.

9¼ in. — Line 1 = 59½ inches long — 7 in.

13½ in. — Line 2 = 51 inches long — 7 in. — 35 in.

9¼ in. — Line 3 = 59½ inches long — 7 in.

13½ in. — Line 4 = 51 inches long — 7 in.

78 in.

QUEEN-SIZE HEADBOARD

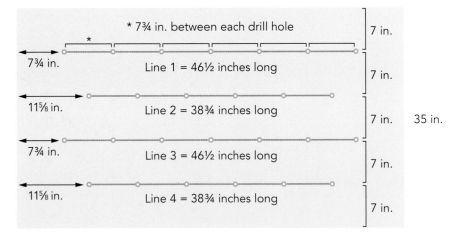

* 7¾ in. between each drill hole — 7 in.

7¾ in. — Line 1 = 46½ inches long — 7 in.

11⅝ in. — Line 2 = 38¾ inches long — 7 in. — 35 in.

7¾ in. — Line 3 = 46½ inches long — 7 in.

11⅝ in. — Line 4 = 38¾ inches long — 7 in.

62 in.

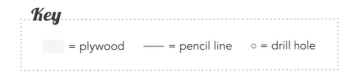

Key

= plywood   ——— = pencil line   ○ = drill hole

FULL-SIZE HEADBOARD

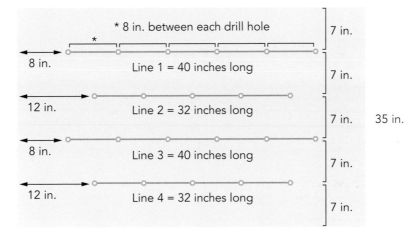

* 8 in. between each drill hole

7 in.

8 in.   Line 1 = 40 inches long

7 in.

12 in.   Line 2 = 32 inches long

7 in.   35 in.

8 in.   Line 3 = 40 inches long

7 in.

12 in.   Line 4 = 32 inches long

7 in.

56 in.

TWIN-SIZE HEADBOARD

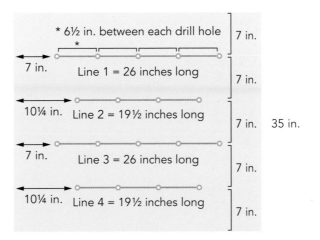

* 6½ in. between each drill hole

7 in.

7 in.   Line 1 = 26 inches long

7 in.

10¼ in.   Line 2 = 19½ inches long

7 in.   35 in.

7 in.   Line 3 = 26 inches long

7 in.

10¼ in.   Line 4 = 19½ inches long

7 in.

40 in.

Flower (for Business Card Holder, page 125)

paper airplane pilot

Heart (for Valentine Tablecloth, page 170)

Snowflakes (for Christmas Tree Skirt, page 191)

Snowflakes should be printed at 125%

Index

Italicized page numbers indicate photograph of completed project.

Notes

Notes

Notes

Notes

Notes

Notes